WOMEN THRIVING FEARLESSLY
for
Mothers

A bold collection of true life stories from Mothers
who dare to say what other Moms are thinking

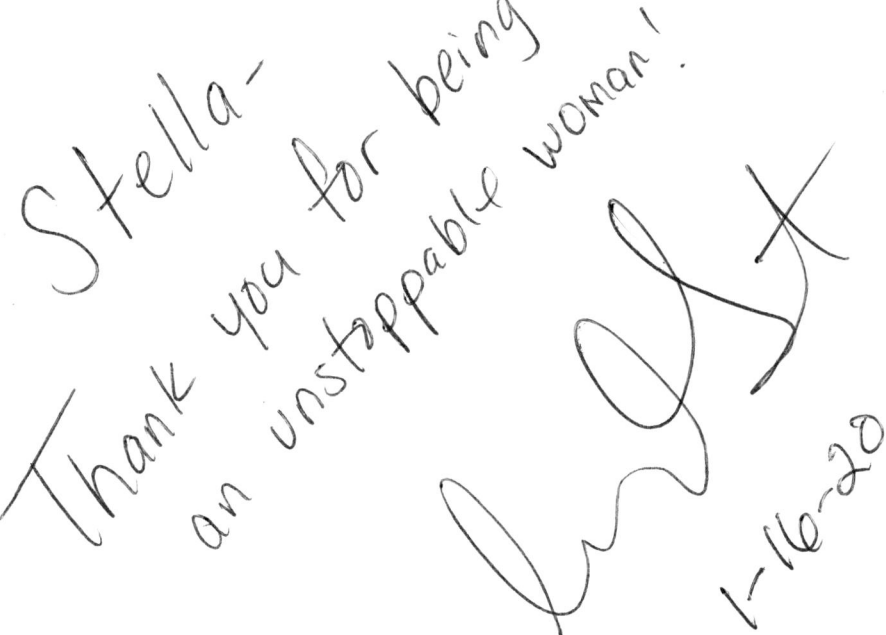

Other books available in the Unstoppable Publishing's Library:

The Secrets to Being an Unstoppable Woman
Roll up your sleeves, make no excuses, and get what you want!

10 Ways to Prevent Failure (Audio Book)
A straightforward guide to help you stay focused on attaining your goals.

Starting Today
365 Quotations to stimulate, inspire, and enhance your personal growth.

The Unstoppable Woman's Guide to Emotional Well-Being
A book for women written by 23 female authors, coaches and professionals.

How to Write & Publish Your Book NOW!!
Step by step guide to put you on the fast track to becoming a published author.

Success Guide for the Unstoppable Entrepreneur
Straightforward guide to help new business owners and entrepreneurs excel in their business.

If You Leave, I Will Kill You! – Getting Off the BEATEN Path of Domestic Violence

Women Thriving Fearlessly Volumes 1, 2, 3
Courageous stories of women who found a way to thrive through life's toughest situations

Women Thriving Fearlessly in Business

www.TheUnstoppableWoman.net

© **MMXVIII** All rights reserved. No part of this book may be reproduced or transmitted in any form or by any means, electronic or mechanical, including photocopying, recording, or by any information storage and retrieval system, without permission in writing from the author.

TABLE OF CONTENTS

Chapter 1 – *My Legacy of L-O-V-E*...................................7
　　Claudia Chavez

Chapter 2 – *Raising "Little Ms. Independent"*...................21
　　Cynthia Fitch

Chapter 3 – *The Impossible*...................................35
　　Felicia F. Clark

Chapter 4 – *Embracing My Strength*...................................49
　　L'Vonne McMillan

Chapter 5 – *Motherhood – A Piece of Cake, But Not Really*...........59
　　Maggie Bockai

Chapter 6 – *Baby Mama Drama*...................................69
　　Paula J. Shelton

Chapter 7 – *Two Motherhoods*...................................81
　　Sandy Oprondek

Chapter 8 – *Mother's Journey from Step-Monster to Step Diva*....89
　　Terrie Vanover

Chapter 9 – *Blueprint of Blended Families*...................................101
　　Tracy M. Sostand

Chapter 10 – *Half a Dozen, Only Children!*...................................109
　　Tricia D. Dunn

Chapter 11 – *How to Breathe When You Have No Breath Left*..123
　　Vicki Walker

1

My Legacy of L-O-V-E

*Mothering my children through a divorce
as I stepped into becoming a healer.*

Claudia Chavez

 Claudia Chavez - Honored to be a mother of 3 amazing and talented young adults, blessed to be a grandmother to one lovable grandson and granddaughter on the way.

Claudia was born in a small town, S.L.P. San Luis Potosi, MX. At the young age of 3, she was abducted from her home town and brought to live in the U.S. with her two older sisters and father.
She was molested as a young child and had to deal with many issues of blame, shame and low self-esteem, especially being brought up in a very strict Catholic school setting.

Her greatest life experience was becoming a mother, as her children were the catalyst to begin a healing that would ignite generational traumatic healing. She dealt with divorce, went bankrupt, became homeless and through it all, she persevered. She had to learn how to forgive herself and practice the legacy of LOVE.

Claudia's greatest teachers have been the children in her life. She became an Early Childhood Teacher, worked with special needs children and had the bonus of being a nanny. As a Qigong instructor and her experience with energy work, she embraced, and continues to embrace helping others understand more about how our own energy and the energies of others affect our every day.

Her learning and life process of self-healing has assisted her to thrive through reading, attending workshops, working with coaches, spiritual healers, understanding energy and experiential work that has lead her to become an NGH Certified Consulting Hypnotist, Peak Performance Coach, Wealth from Within Instructor and Spiritual Minister.

Speaker & Author
Phone: 708-765-8432
Website: http://www.claudiachavez.org
VIDASOL, LLC.

My legacy of L-O-V-E

During my childhood, I had friends of all ages. I seemed to be the go-to person when someone had a problem or just wanted to get something off their mind. Even as a child, I remember longing to be a mother, playing house and teacher were my favorites. I had always been curious as to why children behaved as they did and I couldn't fathom why people rejected them or hurt them. You see, as a young child, I was molested and had to deal with many issues of my own, blame, shame and low self-esteem, especially being brought up in a very disciplined Catholic school. I had also found out that I had almost been an orphan, so my own curiosity grew. Why wasn't I wanted? What was wrong with me? Meanwhile, I was also being brought up in a very strict Hispanic culture, a single dad raising three daughters was a great challenge in this new world. I continued to struggled in my youthful years, I learned very early on to be a people pleaser and kept everything safe and comfortable knowing I would at least have my security needs met. All I needed to do was to keep quiet.

I married my grammar school sweetheart after many years of ups and downs, I settled. I was married at the age of 26, and two months later I found out I was pregnant. This came to us as a big surprise! I thought, this is one of the most wonderful miracles I have ever experienced. I simply felt blessed and confused all at the same time; we had started with rocky marital problems, but I chose to stay for the sake of my son and weather it through.

Fast forward fourteen years later as I was about to move through a spiritual awakening. I had been blessed with my oldest son who was 14 at the time, my other son 12 and my daughter 7. My life was very full and busy with 3 active children - running to and from activities, running a pizzeria, and vacations here and there. There was a wonderful close knit family from my husband's side, which consisted of weekly weekend family reunions, a beautifully built new home, a sweet adopted puppy and a hard ever ready workaholic-husband. I was the very supportive wife and mother.

It seemed to be a real ideal life, right? NOT!

My life came to a sudden HALT after reading my son's words, "If I were to die, it would not matter."

My oldest son, Nick was around 14 years old at the time. One early morning, I happened to stumble across a letter along his bedside. It read, "If I were to die, it would not matter." I knew he was hurting deep down inside. He had been struggling in middle school, wanting to fit in with the wrong crowd, trying hard to be everyone's friend, being bullied by peers, teachers and his parent. He began having anxiety attacks on top of his allergy/sinus infection episodes that enabled him from doing school work and staying home numerous days to recover. His teachers were supportive in his younger years. However middle school was a whole new ball game as he prepared to enter High School, it began to get even more challenging. There was lots of pressure and expectations from school, peers and home life.

I began to ask myself, how could he write these words? What was I doing wrong as a mother? What didn't I see clearly? What was really the root cause? How did I miss the signs that he was struggling this deeply?

It's all about the L-O-V-E Y'all

L-Learn to Love yourself and relearn to listen to the still voice inside YOU! I found out I needed to learn how to LOVE myself, unconditionally! I was caught up in my own little world, keeping myself so busy that I would not think about those deep dark feelings, crying myself to sleep. My marriage had its ups and downs, and we had finally hit some deep downs.

I was tired of trying to change him. I felt depleted. I was numb. I was in a deep depression myself; I was really good at what I call coping or shoving it under the carpet. I was tired all the time; I was a 24/7 mother, giving all my time to my children and everyone around me. My health began to deteriorate. We would have weekend parties, friends, family and/or neighbors, somehow there was always some kind of drinking involved.

I began to drink more on the weekends because "if you can't beat them, join them," right? This allowed me to escape the pain temporarily. However, this was my big wakeup call; I couldn't do this any longer. I knew that everything my children experienced would remain as an imprint in their mind as acceptable behavior, and it would create their belief system where they would operate their whole life from. This was my biggest obligation - not to repeat the cycle. I had to rock the boat and get way out of my comfort zone. The silence was not a solution any longer. Now my children's lives were at the forefront, and mama bear needed to come out.
I had to start a healing process for myself to become a better mother and advocate for my children. I began to listen to my own knowing - that intuitive voice within me. I knew it was the beginning to heal from a mind, body, spirit connection. I began to meditate, stopped the alcohol, changed my diet, became a vegetarian, practiced pilates, took care of my body, and began to seek for solutions through spiritual books, online spiritual teachers, and began to attend workshops. My very first workshop was Dwayne Dyer's. It was a powerful event, and it became very clear, I was on a spiritual quest, and I was scared and confused.

I started to listen intently; I mean really listen to my son's feelings and his needs as to what was the root cause of his sadness. He was a preteen going through puberty years. I had forgotten how sensitive my son was. He has such a big heart, and he is a gentle kind soul. Life at this time was so much pressure for him. I was so not paying attention to his emotional needs. I was barely keeping myself in a good place; I had checked out.

I had decided to heal with my son and not have him feel like he was damaged. He had struggled in his younger years with the labels of ADD, and I knew that medicine was not the answer. I had decided that I would fight for him to learn how to cope without medication, so I worked with his teachers and counselors. I was an Early Elementary school teacher, and everything I had learned about children was not happening here. This was not in our textbooks. Help!

I started asking questions and seeking solutions. I was steered toward various specialists, Neurofeedback Specialist/Counselors, a Chinese Herbalist Doctor, Psychologists, a Chiropractor, and lots of family and friends support.

I remember setting up a meeting to talk with one of my son's teacher's to talk about what was going on in the classroom and how Nick was being affected. Before the end our conversation, it turned around on her, and she opened up about her son and her challenges, tears streamed from her face as she told me her struggles.

I sat and listened intently, when she was done, she reached over and gave me a big tight hug and said thank you for helping her. I stood there like, "What did I do?" She said that, "What you just did," the energy of her conversation had shifted completely.

She explained more about energy as I was just a newbie on this topic.

I was awestruck, I really didn't know what she was talking about, but I genuinely accepted and said I was glad I could help. I walked out of that schoolroom on such a high I had never experienced this feeling before. I asked myself, "What the hell did I just do?!" I wanted to learn more! I wanted to help more people. This was when I got introduced to understanding the power of the mind and a tool called hypnosis.

I knew I loved my children, as each child was born, they each filled a part of my broken heart with love. I had a healthy mother/child bond with them. However, I know I struggled with being the best of one. I was seeking validation from the outside world. I had sacrificed my happiness and I had learned how to live in a toxic relationship.

This was the Root of my son's pain. He longed for a relationship with his father and probably looking at it from this space, he was even longing to reconnect with his mother who had checked out and was sleepwalking and following his father's ways.

Spiritual Awakening leads to a Spiritual Divorce

How could this be happening?! I just remember going to sleep to one of Oprah's late-night episodes, where she describes, verbal and mental abuse and I had an aha moment but refused to really do anything about it. It had to get so ugly at the end I eventually had to deal with another abusive episode. He was determined to make this relationship work, even though I had checked out. I went into some kind of shock! I couldn't believe this was me, was this really happening, it felt like a really bad dream. Did I really create this for myself?

My heart was broken, my spirit was broken, there was no understanding in this space for me to grow. Looking at it from here, now, I stepped into the zone I had to get out!

> *"Peace cannot be kept by force; it can only be achieved by understanding."*
> -Albert Einstein

O- Optimize my E-motions

I had a choice, A) I could get caught up in this spiraling toxic emotional drama, again and again and keep playing the victim card, feeling sorry for myself, allowing my children to hear our constant fighting or B) I could speak my truth and use these emotions and convert them to productive energy to start creating a happier and more fulfilling life in a new paradigm for me and my children.
I chose B. I stepped into the zone. I deserved to be happy! I took all this negative energy and used it for good. I used all the resources I had and put some blinders on and just kept moving. I didn't look back. I took back my life!

For a year, I moved four times, in and out of homes, from my cousins, renting on my own, being homeless to my aunties home, to finally a place of my own. I had to file bankruptcy, had no job, a pending divorce and pretty much lost everything. So, I went back to teaching, became a nanny, and I tapped back into remembering that very special "aha" moment, the energy experience I had with that teacher.

Dared to be the Healer of my own Life
I was on the path to personal healing and in high desire to

find some relief as I sought the world of spiritual healers and I became more curious on this whole new world of Homeopathic Healing modalities. I came across the practice of Qigong, and I fell in love with this beautiful gentle practice, and in no time I became a certified Qigong Level 1 instructor. Meanwhile, my divorce was final, and my ex was remarrying. One closed door as another one opens.

The curiosity of the "What the hell did I just do?" moment was revealed to me after I attended a women's empowerment program. I claimed out loud my I AM... moment. "I AM a HEALER"... I yelled out loud. What the hell was I saying? Where did that come from? I had no idea what to do with this idea; I decided to just roll with it. This propelled me to nurture and blossom into my new upgraded Identity.

I had decided I was going to become a Certified Hypnotist, I didn't have the money, but I trusted somehow I would find it. At that particular time, I had been working for this loving family the Foertsch's, as they had taken me in as their nanny and as one of my nurturing supporters, they believed in me and loaned me the money. I headed out to surround myself with like-minded people, hypnotists, energy healers, EFT practitioners, Reiki masters, Naprapaths and other healers.

I began attending Larry Garret's healing center in Chicago. This is where I would meet my teacher Linda Williamson C.H. I knew she was the one; she spoke my language, and her healing story caught my attention.

V- Vision What do I envision? What do I want?

My oldest son began to have panic attacks again; he'd

always have these episodes when he visited me. He was being told that I was doing the devil's work through hypnosis. Every time I knew he was coming to visit me I would go into a panic and would spiral into feeling like there was nothing I can do to help him. I offered to use some of my breathing techniques and visualizations like we used to do when he was younger, but he refused. I felt helpless.

I remember sharing with my teacher, tears rolling down and my voice choking up with all that was going on in my life. After class, she would sit me down and look me straight in my face and ask me, "Claudia, what do you want?" I had to really think about this I had to get out of the state I was in and flip that switch. I had learned that it was all about the vision and using all of my senses to create it and believe it as if it was already happening. Now, this was easier said than done. So, I took a moment, took a deep breath, closed my eyes, as I went into a quiet trance and responded to her and said, "I want my children to see that I am doing good in the world, my son healed from his panic attacks, my ex to respect me and acknowledge my work, to continue co-parenting with me in an amicable way, and financially continue supporting his children." Then she would say, "Okay now, stretch that, exaggerate it!" I proceeded to stretch out of my comfortableness. "That my dad would also accept and respect my talents and work and that all of my family would be supportive and that they would accept me as a healer that I was becoming." WOW! "And so it is," she replied.

> "Create the highest grandest vision possible for your life, because you become what you believe."
> - Oprah Winfrey

Now fast forwarding eight years later. That's exactly what I have created for myself. Taking it one step further, my son who believed I was a doing voodoo work, was recently married and asked me to be the honorary minister for his wedding. Now that was a BONUS Expansive for sure.

E- Expand Your Identity/EYI

The E stands for expanding yourself to be your very best and new self as a mother, grandmother or any other leadership identity you would like to elevate yourself to be. As I expanded my identity, I learned how to heal my own life, this rippled onto my children, and this gave my children permission to do the same for themselves. Take time to nurture and treat yourself to the  experiences that make you happy, excited for life, seek your purpose and live it, breathe it and speak it out loud no matter how weird you think you are, your children, or anyone for that matter. It gives them an opportunity to be their own authentic, unique and empowered self. Let them know your fears and if you fall, tell them about it, and what will you do differently next time. Accept and embrace your mistakes; this is how we learn and succeed in life. I had to replace this whole sacrificial, self-sabotaging, obedient belief system and replace with an upgraded belief system of learning how to love myself, treat myself well and toot my own horn. I had to practice and use positive words and thoughts to amplify the person I was becoming, fearless yet kind, confident yet giving, compassionate with boundaries.

This gave my children an opportunity to create their own belief systems that best served them. Every time you get out of your comfort zone you expand your identity. Your children are watching! Play and interact with your children no matter what age;

find a common interest and be in that moment with them. If it feels really out of sorts then you are in an uncomfortable state. It takes three days to give up a bad habit and start a new one, and three weeks for it to stick and 90 days for a full upgrade of an identity. Our children come with their own unique thoughts, talents, and gifts - nurture and embrace them. LOVE them unconditionally no matter what. Love heals all! I truly believe we are in a process of healing generational wounds and our children are here to teach us and lead us, once we listen.

My greatest purpose in life has been my children. I realized as I was reflecting on this chapter of my life, that my son was mirroring my needs. As I helped him heal and find his place in this world, it took a whole lot of upheaval to get to this greater version of our lives. He has a closer relationship with his dad, he is a responsible father and husband, and has found a career at which he is really successful. At  different times and different experiences, every one of my children has helped me see through their eyes and walk through challenging life moments, I am truly honored they picked me to be their mother. We are all natural born healers to heal our own life if you dare.

I've read that saying, "Some people come into your life for a day, a moment or a lifetime, they all have a purpose." I am really grateful to my ex for being a great provider; I was blessed to be a mother and to be a stay at home mom watching my children grow and being loved by them - priceless and now blessed to be a grandmother, bonus! ;) Thank you!

Blessings to all of you out there going through any struggles.

My ex and I have a good co-parenting relationship; we are both better parents and people, my other children have a healthier and closer relationship with their father and extended family, abundantly blessed!

> *"Choosing to live in the legacy of LOVE, made it possible to live the abundant **I'm**possible vision of my life."*
> *- Claudia Chavez*

2

Raising "Little Ms. Independent"

How I survived key life-changing moments raising an open-minded headstrong millennial.

Cynthia Fitch

Cynthia Fitch, a Chicago State University Alum, is a very seasoned accounting professional with over 20 years experience in accounting, auditing, financial reporting and management. She has worked for several notable companies and CPA firms including the former Big 6 Firm, Arthur Andersen. She is also a former instructor for Sawyer College (IN), where she taught Principles of Accounting and Business Math. She is a registered CPA in the State of Illinois and an active member of the Illinois CPA Society.

She is currently the CFO for Gareda, LLC, which provides home maker services for the elderly and disabled including veterans. She is also President of S.C. Fitch Enterprises, Inc. which promotes books and events focused on financial and relationship enhancement. The company also owns Amateur Sports News Network, founded by her husband Steve, which is an online media magazine covering youth athletics in the Chicagoland area. She serves as a Commissioner on Matteson's Parks and Recreation Commission and as the Hospitality Coordinator for the Bloom Mentoring Ministry at Victory Apostolic Church.

Cynthia is published author of two books. She's a contributing author for The Unstoppable Woman's Guide to Emotional Well Being writing Chapter 20, "Your Map to Financial Prosperity." She is also the creator of the book and romance enhancement product, "The Erotic Cookie Jar," which provides guidance and a fun and adventurous tool to improve intimacy and romance. After being married for 25 years, this product has become a catalyst for her mission to help as many couples keep their relationship spicy and stay together.

www.scfitchenterprises.com
www.TheEroticCookieJar.com
cfitchcpa@sefitch.com
708-201-1781

Not for My Child

This childhood sucks!!!!! I had to learn early on to adapt to life's changes as I was moved around from my Mom's to my Dad's house, back to my Mom's, then to my sister's house, back to my Mom's, then back to my Dad's, to my Aunt's, and then back to my Dad's. I was forced to change grammar schools three different times, and all of this was before I made it to 8th grade. I knew that my family loved me, but there were times when I couldn't escape not feeling at peace. Everywhere I went, I felt like the extra that didn't fit in. I knew that my mom loved me, but she couldn't take care of me due to illness. I knew that my sister loved me, but I knew she had her own family to take care of and really didn't need someone else to have to take care of.

Staying with my dad, stepmom, and stepsister was another situation. I'm sure they loved me, but I still felt like I was an obligation more than loved and wanted. While they tried to treat us the same, especially with chores and providing essential needs, the adoration, love, and being there for me emotionally or for support in events & activities, etc, not so much. While in school, I was part of the honor society, National Beta Club, PomPon, and Band Flag Girl. I do not recall my parents being at any of my events or being at any of the games to see me perform.

I vowed that I when I had my child, I would make sure he or she would have a stable loving and supportive household. Our love and support would never be questioned. So I prayed and put together my plan to make this happen. I was blessed with an amazing man to spend my life and raise my child with. I thought I had my plan together, but nothing could prepare me for this next chapter called "Motherhood." There are many books on it, but nothing prepares you for your version of it. It's different for everyone but believe you me, it's an emotional rollercoaster ride.

Blessed Intro to Chicken Little

The inside joke about how my Jaz got here was that she was conceived when we christened our first home. It's possible that it's true as she was born about nine months later. I just remember that I had a myriad of mixed feelings when I found out. What in the world am I going do with a baby and what kind of mother would I be? I'm sure I'm not the first person to ask this question.

After a pep talk from my good friend, I became excited to tell Steve. Now all I have to do is find a creative way to tell him. I know, I'll make him go on a scavenger hunt. I went shopping for a few baby related items like a rattle, a baby shoes, and then the test in a jewelry box with a bow on it.

When my hubby came home from work he had a note waiting for him posted on the door. "Please follow all directions once you enter this door." He was directed to put his work stuff on the couch and was given several baby related questions and an item to grab from several locations around the house. The scavenger hunt led him up to our bedroom with a basket full of baby stuff, and the last place was to look under our pillow. There was a box with a bow and a note saying "Hope you are ready for a wonderful gift." Inside the box was the POSITIVE PREGNANCY TEST! I will never forget the look on his face. He was so very happy. Hey had tears in his eyes and a huge smile on his face. He just grabbed me and we both just cried for joy. Nine months later we had our beautiful, tiny baby girl affectionately nicknamed "Chicken Little."

Jaz's childhood was basically a breeze, filled with recitals, cheerleading, sports and sleepovers and of course a few broken bones and bruises. We made sure she was loved and supported and in return she really didn't give us many problems. Fast forward to adolescence. This is where it starts to get interesting.

Are We Clear?

Let me start this section by saying that I am firmly against child abuse, emotional or physical. That being said, I do indeed agree with the bible when it comes to discipline. I was lucky in that I raised my Jaz to be like me and prefer positive attention rather than doing stupid things to get negative attention. We rarely had to spank her as a child. Most of the

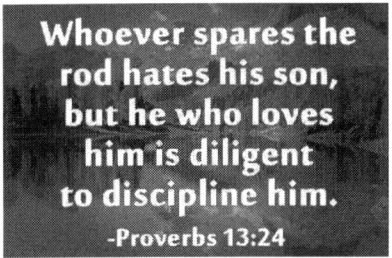

time we were able to discipline her with verbal correction, but in a strong tone. But as with most kids, there were a couple of times I had to, as we parents say "Get in that butt!" There was one time in particular when she was in that tween stage when they start feeling themselves, and their smart mouths make you want to lose religion. This particular day, I scolded her about not cleaning her room and stopped her from going out with her friends until she did and she got to mumbling something smart under her breath which of course led to our having a verbal altercation. I raised my hand to pop her butt, and she raised hers to block me but accidentally hit me. Needless to say, I tore her butt up!!

After this incident, we never had to have that conversation again. She got it. Her mom was crazy, and she could not beat her even if she tried. A wise play mother of mine told me long time ago. When you get to the point in raising your child and they try to test you, you have to make it clear that you are CRAZY and would take them out if they ever raised their hand to you. Although my daughter never raised up again, I made sure she was clear on my position with her.

One day I had a self-defense instructor come to the house to give her and I lessons to protect ourselves. After an hour or so of learning, we were tested by him. We had to show him what we learned by being able to overcome our opponent by sweeping their feet and applying the right pressure to get them to the ground. First, we practiced the move on him then we had to take turns trying to get each other to the ground. She tried to get me on the ground but struggled. When it was my turn, I swept her feet and put her on the ground and held her there. I looked her in the eyes and said "Are we clear," she looked up at me and said, "Yes Mama." She was a pretty good kid. It was rare that we had any issues out of her. We pretty much only dealt with normal stuff, periodically not completing chores that were assigned, putting her beefs with people on social media, and that ever so common, smart mouth and attitude. We were even lucky that we didn't deal with her breaking curfew without calling or deal with her sneaking guys in the house like some parents I know have dealt with. Yep, besides having a major temper like her aunt (she hates when I say that), Jaz was a delight.

The thing that I am the proudest of and love about my Jaz is that she is very thoughtful and affectionate. (Like her momma, of course! ☺) She was always doing very thoughtful things for us and others like helping out her friends and teachers. Yes, I said teachers. Believe it or not, my daughter actually listened and implements much of the advice her dad and I gave her.

Teen Turmoil

"Your mother had better get ready for that T-Shirt!" That's one of the many threats these little bad ass girls at my daughter's high school posted online to Jaz and her boyfriend. You probably didn't understand that threat, as I didn't until I saw the picture that went along with the post. The T-Shirt had "Rest In Peace" on it.

One of the girls was beefing with my daughter's boyfriend for doing something very stupid on social media. He reposted and commented on some inappropriate photos. Unfortunately, being a good girlfriend, my sharp-tongued child had plenty to say in defense of her guy which made his problem her problem and now our problem.

Back in our day, when you had a beef with someone, you would meet up after school, have your confrontation, verbal or physical and nine times out of ten the beef was settled or squashed the next day. Sometimes when beefs were discussed face to face, often it was discovered that the whole thing was a misunderstanding. Nowadays with folks being bolder and meaner than need be due to hiding behind a computer, many beefs are escalated to something folks don't come back from. Basic beefs turn into outright war and cyberbullying and both can lead to serious injury and in some cases, death. This is why this T-Shirt threat sent chills down my spine and shook me to my core. I remember being on the phone with my husband and other family members all the way to work, trying to contain my fear turned anger. I went from, "I hope this thing doesn't escalate to a physical confrontation," to "I WISH a MF would hurt my baby!" I'm sure any parent would feel this at least for a minute, no matter how Christian or spiritual you are. I made it a point to pray for the wisdom to handle this thing so that there is a positive outcome and also for the resources to deal with this situation to protect my daughter if it didn't. We decided to put together a strategy to handle things on three fronts depending on how things went. 1) Diplomatic and spiritual by praying and setting up a meeting with the school and all of the parents of the kids involved. Our goal was to let everyone know what was going on so that appropriate control at school would be put in place and parents could hopefully get their kids in line, including us.

2) Contact our friends in law enforcement and attorneys to assist us if things go left.

3) Contact those friends and family who you only call when things go left, just in case we need to lose religion.
I know some would say we shouldn't think that way, but as a mother, when you are talking about the survival of your child, and there is a choice between my life, my baby's life, or yours....well you know the rest! Thank goodness prayer worked!

There are two lessons here:
1) Do not post or repost inappropriate photos or comments on social media unless you are open for a fight or prepared for the consequences. Just because you were not the one to start the negative posting, contributing to the spread of it can still get you arrested if the pic posted is illegal or can simply get your butt kicked or worse.

2) Teach your child to make sure they have a good relationship with their teachers so that if they are ever in a bad situation, they will have someone who will back them up or vouch for them even if they have done something wrong.

> The Negative affects of social media:
>
> * Invasion of privacy
> * Reduced quality time with family and friends
> * Lack of productivity/ Loss of job
> * Poor School performance
> * Increased Risk of obesity
> * Increased risk of sleep disorder
> * Exposure to scams, hackers, identity theft, fraud and virus attacks
> * Possibility of addiction disorder

Sexual Experimentation

With movies, the internet, and so many other venues that bombard our youth with sexual innuendo or activity, these millennials have become extremely numb, open-minded, moral-less, cavalier, and tolerant, to say the least about love, romance and sex. What we considered as extreme or hushed behavior in our day is normalized activity and discussed almost daily with this generation.

My daughter has always had some little boy who called himself liking her and usually had some kind of kiddy relationship going on with one of the boys at her school, so we never thought about sexual experimentation or any of those complicated labels being an issue in our household. Even after a devastating breakup in her junior year of high school, with her boyfriend of two years, she eventually rebounded and befriended another nice young man who took her to her homecoming dance.

After a while, she began to get tired of him as his maturity level had not caught up to hers and her experiences. She was driving and working at this point and was used to being treated and dated a certain way. She often told me about her issues with him and asked my opinion. One day she and I were in the car heading out on one of our famous Mother-Daughter dates, she told me something that blew my mind. She said, "Mommy I'm not seeing that guy anymore. I have something to tell you. Do you promise not to be mad?" I said, "I can't promise that, but I can promise that whatever it is we will work it out together and I will love you." She sighed and said, "I think I like a girl." "What do you mean?" I said. She said, "I am attracted to this girl at work. We've been talking on the phone and hanging out at work and sometimes after and we have a real connection." I struggled to keep my composure and drive the car, but my mind was like how in the world do we deal with this? Hopefully, it's just a quick passing feeling and will go away very quickly. But the more she talked the more involved this situation turned out to be. Did I approve? No, but at the same time, I couldn't be a hypocrite as a few of my friends are, bi-sexual or bi-curious. They all have moved on to live very respectable, and some religious lives and are married with children. Others are very open about who they are and are very good people, and I still consider them friends despite their sexual orientation. So what I was not going to do is ridicule her or disown her for feeling the way she did. There are too many children 6 feet under because their families and society did that. I informed her about Bible teachings on the matter and that she would have to work through this situation and we would be there for her. Lord, I will tell you that it was very hard as there were many tense days and heated conversations about this "friend" of hers. The biggest issue of all is that they were proud and posted their pics all over social media. Our position was firm in that the whole world does not need to witness your life while you figure this thing out. Once again these Millennials and that damn social media had us in turmoil for a bit. Thank goodness after a while their friendship fizzled and ended dramatically.

    She now realizes that that relationship was a big mistake. Right now she's in a serious relationship with a young man she went to high school with. They both hope to eventually get married and have at least two kids.

Lord knows I struggled with deciding if I wanted to share this part of our journey. I asked my daughter, and she said "Yes. I am comfortable in my skin and know what I want out of life and know that I am loved." She said, "You have more of a problem with my experience than I do. It's a decision I made to explore how I was feeling, I regretted it, and now I have moved on." I still wasn't sure if I wanted to share, so I decided to pray on it. It was put on my heart that sharing our experience and how we got through it may help other parents whose kids are wrestling with their identity and sexual orientation.

The lesson here is that it is our job to teach and guide our children to become thoughtful and responsible, law-abiding and hopefully GOD fearing adults.

College Grown
Jaz is now a college student and is doing quite well. She is active in a few organizations on campus, working part-time and maintaining her own apartment and can cook her butt off. Now that she is experiencing a few of the ups and downs that becoming an adult can bring, we have been able to have some real heart to heart conversations and moments. They say that your relationship often improves when your children get a taste of adulthood and move out. I can definitely say that although we had a good relationship before, we are closer now more than ever! We now talk in a way that we never have before. I am now learning who my baby is as a person and I am proud of what I am seeing. The fact that she takes the time to plan out thoughtful gifts like the wall canvas she had made with all of our significant dates on it.

What teen thinks to do stuff like that? I'll tell you who. My Jaz!!! I have also been very impressed with her thought process on some sticky situations and that she is learning to take control of her destiny. Things we used to have to push her to do or not do, she is doing or stopped on her own.

Mom's advice and lessons learned over the years:

- Put your phone away at dinner and focus on the person you are with at the moment. If you have to check it for business or something important, please do so quickly and then put it away. We are losing the ability to communicate and really connect with one another and develop meaningful bonds due to always being on our phones or texting and messaging versus picking up the phone to talk and speaking face to face. Tone, facial expressions and body language play a very important part in communication. Intent and passion gets lost in communication via text and often causes unnecessary conflict or lack of human compassion.

Source: Study Breaks Magazine

- Remember GOD's arrangement. The Husband is the head of the house as Christ is the head of the church. Be very careful who you pick as your head. Make sure that family and God's love and grace is important to him.

- Remember that while the husband is the HEAD of the family (if you are married), YOU have the POWER to turn that NECK in any direction you want.

- Learn how to cook well; although there are many assets women bring to a relationship, this is one that is most often appreciated.

- Forgiveness and communication are key requirements to maintaining a relationship with anyone. No one is perfect and we all do and say things from time to time that hurt others, especially those close to us. Although it may seem impossible initially after an infraction, there can be love and friendship rekindled after forgiveness and communication. After being married for 25 years, and dealing with 10-35 year friendships, I know this for a fact to be true.

- Do not use credit cards unless it's an emergency or for travel plans and you know that you can pay it off in 1-3 months. Practice using your bank card only. Thus you only purchase what you can pay for.

- Marry someone who is naturally kind, thoughtful, and who makes you laugh. Someone who enjoys doing things to make you smile and it is not work for them. This will get you through the rough times and believe me there will be rough times.

- Map out your finances each month, set goals and work your plan. Remember the famous quote: If you fail to plan, plan to fail.

- Take time to learn basic self-maintenance skills such as how to cook, sew, change a tire, change a light bulb, keep a house clean and pay your own bills. (even if you become rich)

- Learn who is who in your town and state. Knowing a few key people can be helpful in certain situations.

- Keep your friends close and your enemies closer.

- Try to practice fighting evil with kindness. I know it's hard, but sometimes you'd be surprised by the results.

In this world of social media and materialism, these two are very important!!!

- Keep your conflicts and personal business off of social media!

- Remember where all of your blessings come from. Always pray, read your Bible and make time to worship and develop your personal relationship with GOD.

I hope our story and this advice is beneficial and will help not only my daughter, mother's raising kids in this high-tech world, but anyone who reads this chapter.

Were we perfect parents? Of course not. Is my mini me a perfect young adult? No, as she has a lot more mistakes to make and lessons to learn. But, the results of what we did so far are looking pretty good!!!!

Love you to LIFE Ladie Jayy!!! . ♥

3

The Impossible

Felicia F. Clark

Felicia F. Clark is an energetic author. Coined, "The Master Story-Teller". Having wrote her first story at the age of 5, she has been writing poetry and short stories ever since. Her poem, "Springtime in June" is published in "Echoes of Yesterday, The National Library of Poetry" (1994). She is the recipient of two "Young Authors" awards from the city of Chicago. Co-author of Women Thriving Fearlessly! Volume 2. And author of Forgive Yourself, Felicia; A Woman's Journey through Chronic Disease, Traumatic Abuse, and the Struggles of Single Parenting.

Although she is a passionate writer, her pride and joy are her three children: Nikolai, Nyji & Tamea. "NikNyTa, you make life more meaningful. You are the very air that I breathe. *I am blessed beyond measure to be your mother."*

"As lovingly as possible,"
~Felicia Faye Clark

Felicia F. Clark
feliciafayeclark.com

"You sleep already?! Wake up, Mom! It's time to get turnt!" Then Nik proceeded to "make it rain" cash over my sleeping body. That's how I awoke one late night. He just got paid and wanted to give me some money. "Thank you so much for all that you do for me. I love you so much." And with a kiss on my cheek, he was gone for a night out with his friends. It still strikes me as weird when I remind myself or tell others (as I always do), that I have a 20-year-old, 15 and 13 year old. You know what? I've always counted how old the children would be when I reached a certain age. I've always had an idea of how it would all be. But, now that reality is right in front of me, and I am in shock. Where did the time go?

I had it all mapped out; I would rule with an iron fist. "My way or the highway!" I pictured myself saying. Yeah right! And it damn sure didn't include them having their own thoughts, opinions, and viewpoints...not against me. The world at large, but not me. "I'm right!" I would say. "No matter how old you are, I AM RIGHT!" It almost seems out of spite when they would go their own way. I find it highly disturbing. I admit, I feel unstable. On shaky ground. But, deep down inside, I am immensely proud. Uncomfortable. But proud. Which seems to be my mantra. I have been highly uncomfortable and proud for a long time now. Nik is a natural born serviceman. He's gone out of his way to help others. For example, he joined the Disaster Relief Team; going to Texas to tear down and help rebuild homes that were ruined by Hurricane Harvey. Nyji makes great YouTube videos and loves to prank others. And Tamea is an overachiever. She attends Northwestern University in the summer. As well as an actress; performing in school musicals every year. And all three of them are activists. They are big about standing up for the underdog.

I often ask myself, "How did I get here?" With what

seemed like a definite future mapped before me, motherhood was an impossibility.

Meeting in the Projects

"She will never have children..." I will never forget the words my neurologist, Dr. Ewa Shamicka spoke. She actually took the trip from wherever doctors live to where I resided at the time, the projects, to tell us that. Well...I'm not being exactly truthful. She came to discuss a new treatment for me (I have a neurological disorder, Myasthenia Gravis) that would improve my quality of life. While giving us the good news, I received the bad one, "no children." Which is something that really hurt me; even at the age of 14. Although I was too young to have to children, being told that I would never have them, was hurtful. In fact devastating. Because I may not have always known what I wanted to be, career-wise. But, I've always known that I wanted to be a mother. I sat in the back room of Bigma's apartment, looking out the 6th-floor window, through tear stained eyes. Besides the cars and buses, I saw people walking with their children. Some holding their hands, some carrying them. There was even a guy with his toddler son straddling the back of his neck, sitting upon his shoulders. What kind of future would I have without children? I thought.

Impossible

"Girl! I think I'm pregnant! My mama is gone kill me!" My friend Samantha hollered into the phone. I was unmoved; she always thought she was pregnant. But, maybe she is this time. I thought. "You should buy a pregnancy test," I advised. "Girl, I don't know how to use those," she responded. "It shouldn't be too hard. I'll do it with you," I said.

Although I was only 17, I wanted a baby with the "then"

love of my life. It didn't matter that I had gotten accepted to Duke University or even the fact that my father had promised to give us girls a home abortion if either one of us had gotten pregnant, I was determined to have a baby. Although I wasn't exactly trying, I wasn't trying not to either. I guess I left it up to fate. But, I never forgot those words the doctor spoke, "She will never have children". Although I was hopeful, I was very doubtful.

Anyhow, Samantha and I took the 10-minute walk to the local grocery store, and grabbed the First Response pregnancy test...fast results, it said... Exactly what she wanted, fast results. So, we grabbed two and went back to my house.

In no time, we were in my bathroom, reading the instructions on the back of the pregnancy test boxes. "See? It's easy," I exclaimed, "Just pee in a cup, put the stick in there, then wait for five minutes. Two lines mean you're pregnant, one line means you're not. Do you want to go first?" " We can go together," said Samantha. "Hell no!" I retorted. "Not like that, I mean you go in your parent's bathroom, and I go in here. We meet back in here. You put your cup on one side of the counter; mine's on the other side," I nodded in agreeance.

Afterward, we placed our cups on our designated side of the counter and went into the kitchen. I remember becoming impatient. Up until then, that was the longest five minutes of my life. I really wanted to see if Samantha was pregnant this time; because I was so sure that I wasn't. After waiting for what felt like an eternity, we both went into the bathroom to collect our sticks from our cups.

"Yes! Yes! Yes! My momma would have killed me! I'm not pregnant!" Samantha yelled, jumping up and down. I, on the other hand, saw two dark pink lines; one for me and one for...my mouth popped open...the impossible.

Sneaky MG

Labor and delivery wasn't particularly as bad as it could have been, thanks to the high-risk pregnancy clinic. There was a great concern that I could die during labor or delivery due to Myasthenia Gravis. After all, I'm not supposed to be under anything too stressful. I could have a Myasthenic flair, which could cause death. It's all very real, but my 18-year-old self didn't believe in it all. I guess all the times that I had been sick was a distant memory. Anyhow, it was mapped out how I would have a comfortable delivery. Don't be mistaken, I did have pain, but due to the epidural, I escaped excruciating pain. When it was time to push, I only felt pressure.

My first son, Nikolai, was born with a trait of MG; passed on to him by me. The doctors were able to tell by the weak cry that he had. They examined him in the hospital bassinet at the foot of my bed, while I looked on. They shook their heads, "Yes," my heart sank. They returned a couple of hours later to re-examine him. I was informed that the MG had passed through. Meaning, he didn't have it anymore. Because the illness isn't strong enough when passed from mother to child, it only stayed for a couple of hours. Even still, I felt extreme guilt... I wouldn't wish my illness on anyone, not even my worst enemy. So definitely not my baby. Despite MG showing up at birth, Nikolai was a healthy child. Although I was young, I was extremely happy. This little person, that God has entrusted me with, depended on me for his care. Things got a little tricky when I started needing plasmapheresis. Which entailed me having ports inserted into the arteries in my chest. Causing me to refrain from holding my toddler because I had tubes hanging out my chest.

The weight of him and/or the fact that he may snag a tube was rather risky. And although I knew all of the consequences, I still made a way to hold my son. I would sit on the sofa, with a pillow over my chest, and allow him to crawl onto me. Meanwhile, rubbing his back.

I tried very hard not to be sickly and deny my son a normal childhood. I didn't want him to worry about my being sick, or the fact that his dad was not in the picture. I had a boyfriend who took on the responsibility of being a father to my son. I worked full-time and was a full-time student. And my boyfriend worked full-time. We juggled getting Nik from daycare and the household duties. But, I guess it was all too much to take on. Because the stress of it all took its toll on me. I became very sick at work; passing out and awakening in the emergency room. I don't remember much, but the fact that I was constantly asked the date and about my son. I soon found out that I was hospitalized for about four days before I remembered the date, and most importantly, my son. I came home after a week with limited vision. Unable to see my baby and boyfriend clearly. Just two blurred figures in the house. I relied on sounds. I would listen to the pitter patter of my son's feet and wish I could see him...see his beautiful little face. Then one day I could. I glanced in his direction as he raced across the apartment floor. That's when I noticed that I actually saw him and not a blur. And it felt like I saw him for the very first time. Unforgettable.

I soon discovered that parenting didn't come easy with MG. Although, it wasn't easy to begin with, having a neuromuscular disorder made it all the more difficult. I would see parents outside with their children, pushing them on the swings, or guiding them down the slide... Not me. At least not half the time. I had to dodge the sun because the heat didn't agree with my illness or the other way around. Either way, there was a disagreement between the two, causing me to be quick about getting Nik down the slide and pushing him on the swing. The rest of the time, I would watch from the bench, or from a spot that I had under a shaded tree; which I would lay a blanket and have snacks and books for me and him to read if he so happened to join me. Which he often did; running back and forth between play. Other times, depending on the heat, we would either wait until late afternoon, when the sun is starting to set. Or not go out at all. Those times would hurt. I felt guilt. I would try to make interesting things for him to do around the house, but to avail. He wanted to go outside. My boyfriend would take him out on occasion. But during this time, we were in and out (more out than in) of a relationship with one another. Therefore, he didn't get to be with Nik as much as before.

Five years later, I gave birth to another son. And then a daughter a year and a half later with my boyfriend. Just like Nik, my son, Nyji was born with traits of MG. Dissolving in a couple of hours. My daughter, Tamea, showed no signs at all. But, the pregnancy with her was a little different than the boys'. My MG was acting up. I felt weak and had horrible migraines. I knew that my baby making days were over. So the day after I had given birth to her, I had a tubal ligation. Just as I had a portion of my woman parts removed, the mental part of womanhood, after pregnancy, reared its ugly head...postpartum depression.

I honestly didn't know what the hell was happening. Although I've heard about it numerous times with all three of my pregnancies, I honestly didn't believe that it could happen to me. After all, I didn't have it with the first two. But, there I was, drinking liquor and crying excessively on the bathroom floor; my hiding place from all that my life had conjured up. So, there I sat, feeling depressed about everything; my career, or lack thereof. Motherhood, my life, everything. All of which I once thanked God for.

Dual Parenting

Between three children, there were two fathers. Nik's father made it made it quite clear that he wanted no parts stating, "I don't want another mouth to feed." Then the boyfriend that had a huge part to play in taking care of him was suddenly not interested in his two biological children that I gave birth to. He was in and out; more 'out' than in. He played games so much my young children became deeply sad. I honestly didn't know how to soothe them when the only thing they wanted was him. But he didn't want to be there…only when it was convenient. I found that we were a huge inconvenience for most of the time.

As I look back on it all, I really don't know which is worst. Having the father of child entirely stay away? Or, go back and forth? I don't know, but I'm leaning towards "back and forth".

I was left alone to raise three children; by myself. I was scared and embarrassed. All sorts of thoughts rummaged through my head: What if I mess up? Everyone is coupled, but me. I ruined my kids' lives. I'm a statistic.

25 years old with an important task; a task that many before me had to pull off. My mama always, "You are not the first, and you damn sure ain't gonna be the last!" I suffered…so my kids suffered. I had a hard time making ends meet. There were hardships with obtaining and managing money. Therefore, maintaining a household was tough. I spent a lot of time going to different food pantries for not only food but diapers and toiletries.

Bitterness consumed me. Although I love my children, I had difficulty showing affection. I cried so much that I didn't want to be touched. Crying, for me, brings back more tears. And I was very strict. The children stayed on punishment for any and everything they did that was considered bad. Between spankings (which don't work) and standing in the corner (which also didn't work), I tried to be as strict as my father, but as loving as my mother. It didn't quite turn out that way. I was a firm disciplinarian and the affection was greatly lacking. The children were even sadder now, because of me. My mother informed that I need to be mindful of how I was treating them. She said, "Is it possible that you are impatient and short-tempered because of their fathers? The children are also a part of you, Felicia." Is that what I'm doing? I asked myself. Thinking about it brings back tears. I decided that I must change this, immediately. No matter what is happening, a child must know that their mama loves them. I started to pray for strength, guidance, understanding, and patience. Most of all, to be a good mother. The type of mother to raise and nurture the kids that have been gifted to me. Everything that I had in me, I was determined to give to my children. And hence, the transition in my parenting began.

THE YOUNG AND THE RESTLESS, BOLD AND BEAUTiFUL

What can I say? My parenting is a little unorthodox. I have a weird sense of humor. I am that parent that would trip their child. Then bandage them up if they became hurt. I love giving them lots of hugs and kisses. And they love bribing me and charging me for them. Well, not my boys, but my girl. My baby, my one and only girl, gives me coupons for hugs and back rubs...but when I run out, I'm assed out until she feels like giving me more coupons.

I taught my kids how to stand up for themselves and

others. My eldest, Nikolai has always stood up for his peers; befriending them; a natural born serviceman. So, when he went off to Texas, without thinking twice about it, to rebuild homes that were ruined by Hurricane Harvey, it all made sense. It's something that he would definitely do. But, to really put his signature on it, he gave me only 30 minutes notice before he hit the road. No preparation, no nothing. Just daring and full of life. That's Nikolai. And true to form, I nearly had a stroke. My second son, Nyji was recently harassed by a bully in school for standing up for a fellow classmate. He's very outspoken. So, I know that there's going to be plenty more scenarios like this. He's not for the bullying of others. He also records videos on YouTube and Instagram on bullying and fairness. Honestly, I'm not too fond of my children having social media accounts and getting involved in other folks drama. But, I must say that I am beyond proud. Then, my daughter, Tamea marched for gun control and Never Again...stemmed by the murders of students at a Florida high school, amongst other events. During this time, I was called on numerous occasions, while at work about her leaving to go protest. It drove me insane because I had to run into the nearest exam room to take the calls. Although I'm uneasy about their choices, I'm extremely proud. I support them. There have been times that I have screamed in silence. But, I will continue to support them. Especially since they are spreading love and positivity.

    I find myself constantly battling between what my parents would have done and what I believe is best for my children. For example, when my daughter wanted to spend the night with her transgender best friend, my mom had a conniption. And I know if my father had been alive, he would have flipped completely out. In fact, my mom said he was probably rolling over in his grave. But, I said "Yes." After all, how can I teach my children how to stand up for humanity and then honor the dumbest of stipulations placed upon sexuality? Anyhow, I guess you can say that I have given birth to activists.

But, they are still young adults, children...

NIK

"Aaaah!" I screamed. Between the hours of 11 pm and 3 am, Nik comes into my room to either converse, mess with me, or simply be next to me. "What is that?!" I yelled. He didn't explain, just waved the thing in front of my face. Once my eyes focused, I realized it was three incense sticks. Then he lit one and gave me a sort of light show. Then he stuck it in a candle holder and left the room.

Although I'd be completely worn out and have to work in the morning, I love when he comes in my room to visit me. Because if it weren't for this, we would hardly see each other.

NYJI

Working in the medical field, I'm on the move five days out of the week. So, quite honestly, my feet become a bit smelly by the end of the day. One late afternoon, after arriving home, I went into my room to get settled. I sat on my bed and took off my shoes. "Whew", I exclaimed, waving my hand back and forth in front of my nose.

"Hey, mom", said Nyji as he walked in. "Ewww, what's that smell?" He asked as he waved his hand in front of his nose.
"What smell?" I asked.
"You don't smell that? Is it your feet again?"
"Huh?' I asked, dumbfounded.
"Really? You don't smell that? You must be immune to the funk,"

he exclaimed as he walked away.

TAMEA

"I am BROKE!!! Pay me, if you want another hug! I'm cutting you off!" yelled, Tamea as she stood in front me, wearing my face, just more beautiful. I remember a time when I would have her in my arms, almost the entire day. Now, I have to beg for them. And, I've haven't received a coupon for one in a while. I think I have been cut off. I have now resorted to begging and bribing. "Tamea give me a hug! NOW!" I would yell. Meanwhile, she has a stern look, with a slight grin. I can tell she's unmoved.

This is the greatest love I've ever known.

What can I say? That raising multiple children is challenging? Well, it can be. But, it is also rewarding. There is never a dull moment. Things can become hectic, to emotional, to downright hilarious in a matter of minutes. Due to each child having their own personalities, you have to wear different masks when you approach them. And depending on the scenario, how you approach them may entail different wording, with the same meaning. After all, fairness is of extreme importance. Trust me, you do not want sibling rivalry. And then there's that old-fashioned phrase, "You love (fill in the blank) more than you love me." You almost can't escape it. Keep in mind that each child is deserving of recognition and praise. To be supported and loved no matter what. It's a rollercoaster that I do not want to get off.

4

Embracing My Strength

L'Vonne McMillan

L'Vonne McMillan has worked with various agencies providing one-on-one instruction and early intervention with clients with various special needs - Autism, Down Syndrome, and Mental Health Disorders. She has a wide range of experience in the Social Services Field as well as Lead Classroom Teacher at various locations. She started providing tutoring services in June 2004, and has had many families utilize her services with the following subjects: General Mathematics, Algebra, Geometry, Reading, and Writing. With this passion, she started the Marie Morgan Educational Center, Inc. The business was placed on hold due to her son's health. Now that Jordan's health is maintained at a better level, she is able to continue with her passion in working with women and children. She is embarking on a future business based from the chapter Advocate for Me. Ms. McMillan's goal is to enhance the lives of others and to make their life more self sufficient with the gifts and talents that have been bestowed upon her as an Educator, Speaker, Dancer, Social Services Worker and now Co-Author. Her mission and purpose is to advocate for others. L'Vonne shares this experience with her two children, family, and friends. Her driving force is providing her children with self sufficiency and to give them the best that she possibly can as a mother.

Email: advocateforme17@gmail.com
Instagram
Lvonne_McMillan
Advocateforme1
Mariemorganeducational

Facebook:
L'Vonne McMillan
Advocate for Me
Marie Morgan Educational Center, Inc

The definition of a mother is:

1. a woman in relation to her child or children.
2. bring up (a child) with care and affection
3. Provider, caretaker, nurturer, homemaker, guardian of a child

When you think of the word mother you see a woman who cares for children. There was a point in my life when I did not want kids because I used to see how cruel this world was to others. As I got older, the clock started ticking and I thought about it but still was undecided. I guess God had that decision all planned for me. I was turning 30 in January and I knew something wasn't right so I went to the doctor and on January 17th 2007 and the doctor confirmed that I was pregnant. I had a big decision to make, I accepted the challenge of motherhood and so my journey began. I had a tough pregnancy and gave birth to a premature baby boy weighing 2 lb to 3oz. My first introduction to Motherhood was very scary and my child was very sick and could possibly die. I prayed and cried every night, 101 days that my baby boy will be okay and alive. He made it and is now thriving 10 year old with some feeding issues but he is a typical boy.

Introduction of Motherhood, Not Easy But Worth It

My second introduction to Motherhood was after I got married we had a discussion about having another baby. I scheduled an appointment with my GYN doctor due to the complications that I had with the first pregnancy, and I wanted to know if this was something possible in the future. My doctor and I discussed the precautions and dangers and what was best for me. I had my regular exam that day and left the doctor's office. I received a phone call from the doctor a few weeks later that my pap smear was abnormal and to come in for a procedure due to possible cervical cancer. I arrived at the appointment and took a pregnancy test, which was a standard procedure, and the nurse came in the room and said you work fast, you were just here a couple weeks ago saying you wanted to have a baby – well, you're pregnant. This was a shock because I was thinking maybe next year we would have a baby, not this year. I was in school and was so far from a way of thinking of having another child. God again had other plans for me. I had to go to the doctors more frequently and due to my history, I had to partake in various classes, discuss premature labor, and I received shots in my buttocks every month during my third trimester. I had gestational diabetes and sciatica which caused me to go on bed rest during the final stages of my pregnancy. My GYN doctor discussed the dangers of me having this baby vaginally due to my first pregnancy, so we scheduled a C-section on November 28th. This C-section was way different than the first one. With the first one, everything was so fast and rushed that I didn't have time to actually realize what was going on. This C-section I could feel everything. I screamed during the epidural and was so nervous about everything. It was all worth it when a hyper loud red baby girl came out screaming into the world. The family was complete and I was done. I was the mother of two children. Ugh, get it together – you got this or don't you?

My Village and Vision

Now the hard part was going to begin. After just getting my schedule together of having a child with a disability, now I have a newborn added to the mix. It was bit of a struggle and she was a feisty one at that. She was the total opposite of my son – she wanted what she wants and at that moment. I had help from family and friends which was a blessing. They helped with picking up the kids and watching them while I worked or took care of other leadership responsibilities. It truly takes a village to raise a child. The provider, caretaker, Mama Bear, and protector kicked right in. I work hard for my kids; I strive to show them what a valuable citizen should be in this world - respectful, goal oriented, and God fearing.

Sometimes I fail at this thing called motherhood. I have this perception of Claire Huxtable from The Cosby Show with a two-parent home, kids, and pursuing a career. I come from a single-parent home, although I know my father and I'm always a daddy's girl. I always wanted my children to be in a two-parent home. I love how Claire was career-driven but her household ran as a well oiled machine. Everyone had a routine: get dressed, have breakfast, go to school, arrive home, homework, dinner, and they had family fun times. The parents, the siblings, and the grandparents all played a role in raising the kids. When there was conflict in the family, they all agree to disagree. Although they all had their own opinions, they looked at the best interest of the family and chose to do what's best for each other. Sometimes in life we have this perception of what our life is going to look like but then reality sets in and things change for the best or for the worst.

Weep or Win

I'll briefly share with you my story of raising two kids and thinking I had the perfect family home. The first few years were that well oiled machine that I described. But my reality set in when I started experiencing changes in my relationship and our finances. It started out very small with asking questions here and there but became bigger when utilities were being cut off and we had to uproot the family numerous times until they were turned back on. And I was still providing, trying to keep the family together. I did what was best for the family and sought outside help. Sometimes when crying for outside help from resources, the staff talked down to me and sometimes I felt belittled. Still I pressed on to make a life for my kids with a two parent home even if it was hell. I remember when I wrote my first chapter in Women Thriving Fearlessly Volume One. I was so excited about the opportunity and my kids were too. But the relationship was coming apart and all we did was argue in front of the kids. I never wanted this type of atmosphere for them. So I shut down and continued to try to keep the family together. We sought counseling but it seemed as though everything got worse. As the mother of two children, I'm very protective over my kids and I want the best for them. I wanted to protect them from hardships, but eventually I had to share what was going on. They went from seeing a mother who had the house clean, cooking, work, and keeping their schedule, to a mom who yelled, cried, stop caring about the house and maintained just a little to get by. I gave up on that Claire Huxtable fairytale. Life threw me through a loop and I was the person who was always the one fixing everyone else's problems.

Tribulation or Triumph

As I write this chapter, we currently lost our house and are staying with the family friend. I am now faced with the one fear that I have always feared for my children, and that is losing a home and our family.

And Still We Rise

I watched what was once a well-oiled machine crumble into nothing and I still had to continue to move everyday as if nothing was wrong. My children and I continue to go to church, go to school, and participate in extracurricular activities with a smile on our faces but my mask hides depression and hurt. I continue to push for my kids' sake. As a mother we give, we give, we give, we give and we give until we have nothing left and we seek to have it replenished. My replenishment was my relationship with God. On the days that I wanted to give up the most on everything - business, leadership, family and friends, God gave me the strength to continue on. My kids and I have grown from this situation. It was clear that I was dealing with financial abuse in my household. I saw myself sinking and didn't know how to control it. I want to be strong enough to hold the pain inside, but now I could no longer hold it. I was crying in front of my children because as much as I tried to keep everything intact with a smile on my face, I had to face the fear of losing it all. I began to doubt my decisions but I pray and ask God to order my steps. This was a new challenge for me - one that I had never experienced because I was always able to fix it before it got to this point. I went to the doctor and they diagnosed me with depression that I was not going to accept. I watch YouTube videos that position me to change my mind set.

I'm that protective mother who has to care for them day in and day out. I told my kids that we will pray through this and I encourage them to say affirmations just like many of my mentors tell me to do. My kids chose these affirmations on their own:

"I am powerful, I am strong, I am a child of God, I can do all things by myself; I can do all things through Jesus Christ who strengthens me." I was amazed at the words that they were reciting.

Forecasting My Future

As I write this chapter I can't tell you what my future holds but I know WHO holds my future for my kids and me. I'm saying yes to this journey of motherhood, and today's journey of advocating for women and children who may experience the same thing that we went through. I found it hard to create a plan for a woman who has a career and an entrepreneur at that. There were no places for me to seek help financially or find stable housing. All I could do was save, but the more I saved the more I had to invest in my kids or my business for it to elevate. I want to empower and find resources for women who are in situations like this and need assistance to hold them up in their time of need.

The storm
I recall this one time my van needed repairs so the kids and I were on the bus for a few weeks. My daughter and I were on the bus and the sun was out. Our stop was coming up and she was excited to pull the string to let the driver know that we were getting off. We stepped off the bus and we were 4 blocks away from my son's school. We turned to cross the street and it instantly began to rain - not just drops of rain...pouring rain, and just that fast the streets were flooded. We did not have an umbrella or a jacket. My daughter grabbed my hand in fear because it was raining so hard we couldn't see. She was about to cry and my head started to hurt. I was lost and couldn't figure out how we got to this point. I took a deep breath and took her hands and placed them around my legs and I told her don't look, hold on to me and I'll lead us. Every piece of rain hurt my face but I had to get to my son and we had to get home. She held on and I pushed through. Yes it hurt, and yes we were soak and wet but I moved through the storm and the rain. We made it to the door of his school and just like that it stopped raining. We left a puddle on the school floor. When the three of us walked out I felt something come over me - that no matter what came my way I pressed on, I pushed on, and I propelled to the end.

    I share this story with you not for glory, not for pity, but for the next woman to know that fear is not an option, failure is not an option. Everyone has a journey, and if you ask me if I would pick this journey I would have told you NO! I can tell you this that this journey has made me a stronger person, a stronger mother, and a stronger human being. It gave me insight on what I see so many families go through and I was now in it. I can give you some steps to prepare for this journey called motherhood. What we sometimes expect might not happen. I'll leave you with these words to continue on in your journey as a mother.

Expectation- Expect good days and not-so-good days.
Encouragement- One thing that got me through when it got rough was to find a group of people to encourage me and most of all encourage myself. We are not perfect, but we are striving.
Every single day- Take one breath in, breathe it out. You feel that? That's a second chance.
Example- Be an example for your children. The hardest thing for me was to control my anger because I instill in my children that you don't fuss and fight. Always choose love. So I have to be an example.
Energy- When all of your energy is gone and you gave it all you could, get your energy and drive from your kids. When they hug you, kiss you, and tell you they love you, take that and let it be your fuel for the next day to grind.

As mothers, we may go through the fire but when we come out we won't smell like smoke.

5

Motherhood – Piece of Cake, But Not Really

Magbundeh "Maggie" Bockai

Abandoned pregnant at 27years of age by her ex-husband, mistreated by her ex mother –in- law, laughed at and teased in elementary school because of the biological name she was given, Magbundeh Bockai and was able to overcome her obstacles and accomplish her dreams to become a nurse.

She was able to Graduate from the School of Nursing at Columbia Union College and received a BSN in May 1997. In addition, she furthered her education and received a MBA in 2011 at University of Phoenix. She was born in Washington D.C. at D.C. General Hospital. She lived in D.C. up until the 4th grade, and then relocated to Maryland. Her family and her roots are in Silver Spring. For the most part of this chapter, it talks about the many obstacles she had to face and overcome. Regardless of her obstacles, she had to focus, be persistent and diligent in order to get through her struggles. As a result, she was able to thrive and be fearless in achieving her goals and dreams.

She hopes this chapter will be an inspiration and blessing to someone who has lost hope and feels helpless. Remember it is not how you start that matters, but how you finish. So don't give up on life. Stay strong and focused. As a result, you will accomplish your dreams once you do.

Email: maggiebockai@hotmail.com
Legal Shield Representative

I Magbundeh "Maggie Bockai," became a Mother on January 26, 2001, when Julian Belay was born. He was delivered at Washington Adventist Hospital at 12:45 pm. Dr. Sheik was the Obstetrician that delivered him at the time. Boy, let me tell you I didn't know what I was getting myself into. My whole life changed when he was born. I was so used to doing everything for myself, but then it became about Him and me.

Julian's father was in Greece at the time when he called to congratulate me while I was at the hospital. Unfortunately, he wasn't there during my delivery, but at least he called. Julian's father is Greek and has lived in Greece ever since he left to go back to his country in 2000. I have been mommy and daddy since Julian was born. His father chose not live in the USA or to take much part in raising him so I did what any responsible mother would do and that is to take care of my son. He was the best present I'd received in a long time. He made me grow up quickly especially at the age of 27.

I started working at PG. Health Dept/Maternal Child Health 4/2000 until 8/2004. I had to get up every morning at 6 a.m. to breastfeed Julian, then drop him off at the babysitter before going to work. This had to be done Monday thru Friday. Weekends were my days off, so I relaxed during that time. I had a dog named Alex who at the time was one my loyal friends. Alex is short for Alexandra. I had her since she was a puppy at eight weeks old. On the weekends I would go for walks with Julian on my chest and Alex on a leash. It was quite soothing, you know. It taught Alex to understand that Julian came first and she was going to have to take her place as the big sister. She actually learned to play that role and was very protective of Julian.

I didn't have much sleep during the week since Julian

would wake up in the middle of the night for me to breastfeed him. There were times when I would give him bottled milk and mix it with cereal just so he would sleep longer at night and not wake up early in the morning. That actually worked until he became about four months old. He began sleeping through the night without any interruptions by the time he was five months.

I worked at the Maxim Healthcare Nursing Agency for years after leaving the Health Dept. I started working at Washington Hospital Center Oct. 2008 till Feb. 2017 as Psychiatric RN on 2Kunit and 2 L unit. I worked PRN which was on – call. I could schedule the shifts I wanted to work based on their availability. I primarily worked night shift from 7 p.m. to 7 a.m. By the time 3 a.m. would hit, I would be so tired. That's usually the time I go to take my break for at least 1 hour. Once I return from break, I would have to pass meds for three hours until the shift was over. Once the shift was over by 7a.m. I had to report to the oncoming Nurses at 7a.m. and then drive home feeling heavy with sleep. I didn't mention that Julian was wide awake most times when I would arrive from work. So I would have to get him ready to drop him off at school before going to bed. Once he got out of school, I had to pick him up from daycare Monday thru Friday.

My sister and brother, along with my mother would help me with babysitting Julian if I needed to go grocery shopping or go to work during the times I would pick up extra shifts. My father would take part as well in babysitting which was really cool.

The task of taking Julian to school and picking him up from school became redundant, so I would need a break sometimes. I actually planned a trip to London when Julian was about six years old. I left him with my mom, booked a ticket to London and stayed for three weeks. It was one of the best times in my life. I got a chance to visit my aunt in London and spent time with her and her children. I learned how to speak British and ate some of their foods. I visited Buckingham Palace, Oxford Circus, and learned how to go through the Piccadilly line on the train. My cousins did a wonderful job showing me around London, introducing me to some of the Pubs and going to the outings that they had. I took part in my aunt's wedding as one of her bridesmaids.

Once I returned from London, I would get back to my routine of taking him to school and going to work Monday thru Friday. I did get a chance to take him with me to Brooke Side Gardens in July of 2010. He went on some of the rides that were designed for a nine-year-old. My mother would come along too for fun as well. We took plenty of pictures at Brooke Side Gardens. I had a wonderful time, you know?

Bitter Sweet Reunion
One night I received a call from Julian's Dad John. He stated, "I want to meet with you and Julian." This would be the first time he would meet up with Julian. We made arrangements to meet up in Germany for the first time when Julian was nine years old. We stayed at my Aunt's house who lived in Germany at the time. His father only saw him for two days while in Germany and then went back to Greece due to an emergency situation that he had to handle. Can you imagine flying all the way to Germany for a vacation hoping the father of your child would be eager to spend time with his son, only tell you that he had to leave on an emergency after only two days?" So we made lemonade out of lemons. Julian and I got the chance to visit the Zoo in Germany, go to a botanical garden and a farm in Germany. It was one the

most adventurous and exciting opportunities we could experience.

I returned to the USA and started back working Monday thru Friday again. However, I felt that I wanted to achieve something more than just having a job. I wanted to feel like my life could be more fulfilling. I visited the University of Phoenix and spoke to a counselor about going back to school for a Master's Degree. The next thing I know I started the program in August of 2008. This was one of the most difficult decisions I had made in my life. I was responsible for working at Washington Hospital Center two nights a week 7p.m. to 7a.m. and pay my mortgage every month. It wasn't easy at all. I had to take Julian to one of my aunt's house to babysit him one night a week and then go to class. I had to bounce him around from staying at my aunt's house to my sister's house or my mom's house. There were nights when I had to pick him up from the babysitter to take him to my mom's house then rush off to work. This routine went on for two years until I graduated from University of Phoenix May 5, 2011, with a Masters of Business Administration. This was one great accomplishment I achieved through the Great Lord Almighty.

> *Jeremiah 29:11 "for I know I have plans to prosper you and give you hope towards your future."*

You can accomplish anything you set your mind to once you set your goal. Despite your obstacles no matter how challenging and difficult it may seem, if you focus on your dreams, you can achieve anything you set your mind to.

Setting Boundaries is a Challenge, But Necessary

My son would stay with me on the weekends but stay with his grandma during the week. One time he stayed at my house, and this kid name Will threw a rock at my window and cracked it. It turned out that this kid was one of the bullies in the neighborhood. His mother had four kids, and he was the oldest. They lived right in the back of my house. Will confessed to throwing a rock at my window one time when he and my son were playing outside. Unfortunately, Julian wanted to get into a fight with him. He told Will, "You know that's my house you messing with, man! Don't be throwing rocks at my house." He had come in the house to tell me what happened and he was looking for something to hit the kid with. I had to calm him down and tell him not to go back outside and that it really wasn't worth fighting that kid. I explained, "He doesn't know any better, and no one taught him how to respect his neighbors and their property. Sometimes the best fight is to be the better person and not stoop to his level and avoid him." Finally I discussed with Julian the importance of maintaining a cool positive mindset. It was imperative that he not retaliate, otherwise we would be dealing with things on another level. I definitely didn't want any fights to break loose, so I calmed him down by talking to him about letting go. Julian decided to listen and didn't go outside that day.

Being a single mom of this teenager, for now, has its challenges. Sometimes he wouldn't want to listen to me when I would tell him things that were for his own good, and he would challenge me and not want to listen. If it wasn't for my brother, his Uncle John, stepping in and assisting me with talking to him to get some sense in his head, I don't know what would happen. There were times when Julian would lie to me consecutively when it really wasn't necessary and I would get so disappointed in him. Uncle John would have to step in and ground him and put him under punishment. Furthermore, he would take away privileges to his phone and not be able to go to the gym at L.A. Fitness. Julian really had a passion for working out at the gym (playing basketball) so being grounded from the gym was a big punishment.

There were times when Julian would stay at my dad's house. My father would take him to his business and teach him about the pharmacy. My father has a pharmacy store in which my sister and brother worked in. Julian would go to the pharmacy on Saturdays to help grandpa. This taught him about work ethics and discipline. My father taught him how to count pills and search for the client's prescription to give it to them when they come to pick up their medication. Julian helped out at least two to three Saturdays a month. In addition, he would help his grandpa with recording funds in the computer on his spreadsheet, fix his computer and cable system when it would break down. My dad felt so proud to have Julian assist him with his tasks at this job. I was so proud myself to see him working with my dad; it brought a sense of relief, comfort, and appreciation for having my father around. My dad had been a true blessing in our lives. He helped fill in the gaps that Julian's father did not fill. I am truly grateful for his time, care and attention. In addition, I would have to include my mom, sister, and brothers for their dedication, love, attention, and assistance in rearing Julian.

So for all you mothers out there that sometimes go through struggles with disciplining your child, try to establish order in your household during chaos. My advice is to believe in yourself as a mother. It's challenging being a mother because you are a teacher, discipliner, and an encourager as well. The things you put into your child or children you get out of it. Stay consistent with teaching your child and disciplining. As time goes on your child will learn to respect who you are and what you are in his/her life. Second, give a lot of love by showing how much you care about your child. The little things you do liked celebrating his/her birthdays, buying toys, and taking them on trips, show them how much you love them, and they will appreciate that when they get older. Finally, don't give up when you have difficult matters concerning your child. No matter what, that is your child and he/she will make better use of themselves if you don't give up on him/her. They really depend on you to grow into the man or woman they're destined to become.

> *Philippians 4:6 "Do not worry or be anxious for anything but in every situation by prayer and petition, with thanksgiving present your requests to God."*

6

Baby Mama Drama

Paula J. Shelton

The youngest of 6 siblings Paula Shelton developed her love of books early on due largely in part to her mother, who was a member of the Book of the Month Club throughout her childhood. In high school her interests expanded into teaching English Literature and writing. It was then with encouragement from one of her teachers that she began to keep a journal, write short stories, and poems. After high school Paula pursued a degree in Business Operations thinking it a more practical route, and spent several years in loan and retail management.

Unhappy with the long hours spent away from her daughter as a retail manager Paula decided it was time for a change and applied for a job as an office clerk with Chicago Public Schools. During her interview when asked what her favorite part of her job was she replied, "Training my staff. I love to teach people new things and to watch the excitement on their faces when they get it. That makes me feel great." That response changed the course of the interview and her life; she was offered a position inside the classroom, which she happily accepted.

She has been with Chicago Public Schools for 8 years and has since earned a degree in Early Childhood Education. Her love of books has remained constant and one she openly shares with her students. It has always been a dream of hers to write a book, but one she never had the courage to pursue until recently. Paula Shelton was born and raised on the south side of Chicago in the Englewood neighborhood. She still resides and works there today.

Paula J. Shelton
Email: sheltonpj@gmail.com

> *Standing there watching as he put my daughter in the car with another woman so many thoughts ran through my mind, but the one I clung to most was, "I should whoop that bitch ass."*

Oh Hell No!

It had only been two weeks since I had left my daughter's father on his knees crying and begging me not to take his child away and here he was at my parents' house expecting me to just hand my daughter over to him for the weekend. To make the situation worse, he had his new bitch in the car waiting outside. My mothers' eyes were burning a hole in the back of my head as I handed him the baby bag. I could hear her thoughts in my head, "I know you not gonna let him take that baby out this house! Fuck him!" As much as I didn't want to let my daughter go with him I knew it was the right thing to do. I understood that in trying to punish him I would only be hurting my child.

Standing there watching as he put my daughter in the car with another woman, so many thoughts ran through my mind, but the one I clung to the most was, "I should whoop that bitch ass." I wanted to snatch her little ass through that window and beat that ass until I got tired, rest and then beat her ass some more. Instead, I watched to make sure that he put the car seat in correctly and gave a tiny wave as he pulled away from the curb. I couldn't bear to hear my mothers' thoughts on the subject, so I went straight up to my room.

I paced the floor out of anger and frustration. I was angry that I had given this man so much of myself. Angry that I had allowed myself to remain in a relationship that was unhealthy and unwanted for far too long, but at that moment I was most angry that the bitch had the nerve to come to my house! I grabbed the first thing I saw, which happened to be a little doll, and began to slam it repeatedly against my dresser until the head popped off and hit me in the eye. I then dissolved into a pool of tears on my bedroom floor.

A few minutes later I got up, wiped my tears and checked my eye in the mirror. As I tended to the swollen scratch on the side of my eye, I realized two things. The first was that I had completely destroyed my daughter's doll, and the second was that I was mad at the wrong person. Here I was pissed off and ready to fight a complete stranger over a no good ass man I didn't want anyway. I was never in a relationship with that girl. I didn't get engaged to that girl. I didn't live with that girl. I didn't spend the last three years of my life with that girl. I didn't have a daughter with that girl. So why was I mad at her? She didn't do anything that he didn't allow her to do. I had no idea what he did or didn't tell her about our relationship so for all I knew she had about as much information on me as I had on her, which was basically nothing.

I made a promise to myself right then and there. I was not going to be some ratchet baby mama. My daughter was my number one priority, and I was going to focus on doing what was best for her. I wanted her to have a good relationship with her father, and I knew that he loved her. So for me, that's what was most important. I knew it might be difficult at times, but I was not going to let that get in the way of my daughter having both of her parents in her life.

That's Just My Baby Daddy

Being a single parent isn't easy. It's a lot of hard work

with many sacrifices. You're constantly worried about your child's well-being and their future. So with all of that pressure and stress, I've never understood why some women deliberately keep their child's father away. It's one thing if it's not a safe situation for the child, but if you have someone who is willing and able to be a part of your child's life, why not allow them to be a part of the parenthood journey? We sometimes put our anger about the failed relationship ahead of what's best for our children. I get it; you don't like that motherfucker, he ain't shit, he just a baby daddy. Guess what? You made a beautiful baby with him, and that baby deserves to have their father in its life (even if he ain't shit in your eyes).

Children growing up in households without fathers or a father figure are 30% more likely to engage in drinking, drug use, and other high- risk behavior such as dropping out of school.

For me, having an open and honest conversation with my daughter's father made it easier. I let him know from the beginning that the end of our relationship was not the end of their relationship. I didn't have the best relationship with my father, and we lived in the same house, so I knew I didn't want that for my daughter. We immediately talked about visitation. I didn't want him to feel like he couldn't see his daughter when he wanted to. I placed no restrictions on him when it came to that. He decided that he wanted to have her on the weekends and holidays and I was fine with that. I only asked that I have her on Christmas day, which worked out fine because he didn't really celebrate Christmas at the time.

We discussed her being around his girlfriend; you remember the one whose ass I wanted to beat until I got tired? Here's the thing. You have to trust that your child's father will not place your child in any danger and that includes the people that they have around them. I knew that he loved our daughter more than anything and that he'd protect her from harm so I had to believe that he wouldn't have her around someone who would harm her. I also knew that no matter what I said, he was going to do whatever the hell he wanted anyway, not to mention that he'd already had her around our daughter while we were still together. Like seriously dude, who the fuck you think you fooling?

I told him that as long as she was respectful of the fact that I am her mother and what I say goes when it comes to the well being of my child, I didn't have a problem with it. Because let's face it ladies, unless you had a child with a monk they're going to be around another woman. What's important is how you handle yourself and the situation because whether you realize it or not, your child is the one who's really dealing with it.

Co-Parenting for Dummies

Co-parenting is defined as sharing the duties of parenting. This sounds great in theory, but in reality means different things for different people. For myself it meant me doing all the actual parenting with all that entails, and his ass basically babysitting on the weekends. I sent a well behaved and beautifully coiffed little girl with her father each Friday evening and on Sunday night got back a disheveled little minion. Her hair was all over her head, her clothes were mismatched and dirty, and she would be acting all kinds of crazy. I swear it was as if I had to deprogram her every time she came home.

Now I know that nobody will ever take care of my child like I take care of my child, but damn you're her FATHER. What the Hell! So I had a conversation with her father about what I felt was a problem, i.e. her appearance when she came home and her behavior. This asshole comes at me with the "don't tell me how to raise my kid" bullshit. Oh okay. That's how you want to handle this? Bet! So I hit him back with the "let me tell you this motherfucker, let my child come home one more damn time looking like she don't belong to nobody and that's yo ass! It won't be me telling you how to raise your child it'll be a judge, and you can believe that shit!" The following Sunday night she came home looking like an angel.

I could have let it go and just accepted the situation as it was, but that would have sent the wrong message. He called me after he dropped her off that Sunday to talk about what happened and I explained to him that I expected him to treat our daughter a certain way whether we were together or not. Allowing him to send her home looking any kind of way was unacceptable. It reflected poorly on us as parents, and he needed to understand that.

Now let's talk about the deprogramming. I raised my daughter in an environment of love, structure, routines, and schedules. That is what children need. They thrive on it. It became very clear that at her father's house, while there was no shortage of love, there was, in fact, a drought in the structure, routines, and schedule department. So after a weekend at her father's house, my little girl came home acting like a different child.

This was so frustrating! Getting her back on schedule, correcting her behavior, and fielding my mother's "she don't do that here" would drive me crazy! Mondays were the worst and Tuesday wasn't that much better either, but by Friday she would be back to her normal self...just in time to go to her dad's house. Fuck my life! Ladies I know some of you know what I'm talking about and you are feeling my pain. I know you have questions too. What did you do girl? Did you cuss his ass out?

The answer is simple. I focused on my child and not her father. I talked to him about her behavior, and he answered exactly how I knew he would. "She acts fine over here." I could have gone off on him, but what would that have solved? I wasn't there, so I didn't know how she acted in his home, nor could I do anything to control it. So I focused on what I could control. I started having conversations with her before he picked her up. I would tell her to have loads of fun with her dad while she was gone and to be on her best big girl behavior just like she was at home. When she came home, I greeted her with, "there's my big girl" to sort of signal the change in behavior that was expected.

While we talked about her weekend we'd prepare for the week by laying out her school clothes, going over homework, tidying up her room, all the things "big girls" do. If she did or said something wrong or inappropriate I'd remind her that it was unacceptable and it was not to be repeated. And yes if it was called for, I'd give her a spanking, albeit not often, be it on the butt or hand I got her little behind when I needed to. I know that some have issues with spanking, but I urge each of you to always do what feels right for you. For me, God said spare the rod, spoil the child, and that felt right. It took some time, but eventually, I no longer needed to deprogram my daughter, she began to make the shift all on her own.

Pick Your Battles

Did I mention being a single parent is hard? Especially if you're trying to co-parent with someone who has a completely different outlook on parenting than you. My daughter's father could not be more different from me when it comes to parenting. This is true of many co-parents. These differences bring about many challenges and the key to overcoming them is in how you address each one. Ladies pick your battles! It was frustrating as hell when my daughter's clothes began to come up missing. First, it was a sock or a pair of underwear, and then it was a shirt or a pair of pants. Once ya'll a shoe was missing. A whole damn shoe! How in the Hell did you lose my baby's shoe?

I would be on the phone heated about my daughter's stuff until one night it was as if that missing shoe hit me on top of my head. I was the only one upset. My daughter wasn't upset because she was a kid. He wasn't upset because he was a man and they just don't worry about stuff like that. His wife wasn't upset because she didn't know what was going on anyway. I was the only fool upset.

So from that moment on, there were daddy's house clothes and shoes and home clothes and shoes. I also started having her pack her bag with me so I could we talk about how to keep up with her belongings. After that things got much better. Yes, there was still a missing sock or shirt now and then, but it was no longer a big deal. We still don't know what happened to that shoe though.

Other issues arose from time to time that warranted a more personal approach, such as the time my daughter's hair started to break off. His wife had asked if she could wash and press my daughter's hair because they were going to attend church on Sunday and I said it was okay. When she came home, her hair was very nice, and I was appreciative of the gesture. From then on his wife would do her for church. Everything was fine until one day while I was combing her hair for school I noticed some breakage. I couldn't figure out what was causing it because I was very careful and gentle with her hair.

The next Sunday night I noticed a smell coming from her hair when I hugged her. I later asked how his wife did her hair for church and she said that she pressed and curled it. I asked if she washed it first and she said no. I had my answer there; she was putting heat on dirty hair, which was causing it to break off. Yeah, I was pissed. I immediately called them and went off about how she had "fucked up my daughter's hair," and she was a "stupid ass" for pressing dirty hair (so yeah I didn't always get the not being a ratchet baby mama part right).

I know some of you are thinking, "Yes, you told that bitch right!" Nope! I was wrong. The fact of the matter is that she was only trying to help. To do a good thing for my daughter and I overreacted. Get yourself a good friend who will point this out to you during your self-righteous recap of the whole ordeal. Shout-out to my girl Camille! I called and apologized to his wife and she, in turn, apologized to me, and we never had any issues moving forward.

This leads me my last point. It only benefits you and your child when you have a good relationship with your ex's significant other, be it his wife, girlfriend, or whoever. What you have to remember is that **you don't want that motherfucker anyway!** Let him be her damn problem! Unless of course, you do still want him and in that case God bless you, let me know how that works out for you. Remember, this is someone your child is going to be around so you'll have to form somewhat of a relationship so that the lines of communication are open and clear. I'm not saying you have to be BFF's, but being polite and cordial goes a long way, and mutual respect is a must.

You Got This!
It was not always easy, and I definitely made some mistakes, but the one thing I did not do was lose focus. My daughter was always my main focus. If something wasn't working, I changed it. If something needed my attention, I attended to it. I spoke up when needed, and I learned to not sweat the small stuff. There will be people in your ear giving advice from all angles, but you have to do what's best for you and your child. Everyone's situation is different. You might have had a different type of "no good" man than your friend, or he might have simply been not good for you, but still a good man.

Either way, understand that a failed relationship should not define the way you parent your children. Our children deserve to have both parents in their lives and if God has made that possible, who are we to stand in the way of it? Remove your hurt feelings and pride from the situation. Speak only positivity and love into the narrative and watch as you, your children, and your life begin to thrive.

7

Two Motherhoods

Sandy Oprondek

Sandra L. Oprondek is a health and wellness coach who has a zest for life, learning and helping people. Her slogan, "Invest in your health for true wealth" became her mantra after seeing her parents and other retirees succumb to debilitating health issues. Instead of enjoying their golden years with travel and leisure, their finances went instead to pay medical bills.

Sandy began researching to learn more about preventative health and found USANA Health Sciences. She left her long, successful career as a financial advisor and is now a USANA Independent Distributor. She educates others about the triad of health - eating better, exercising, and taking quality supplements. Sandy knows this will help everyone live a healthier, happier life, which she demonstrates by sharing her own amazing personal triumph.

Sandy lives in Homer Glen, with her husband, Jeff. The mother of 5, grandmother of 10, and great-grandmother of 1, Sandy is doing everything she can to stay healthy, keep her family healthy, and live the life of their dreams!

CONTACT INFORMATION:
Website: www.sandyoprondek.usana.com
Email: sandy.truehealth@gmail.com
Phone: 708-334-2261

My First Motherhood

My story of two motherhoods begins in the 1970's when I graduated high school and got married soon after. At that time, it was typical to get married very young. My husband and I started a family right away and my first child, a son, was born in 1973. My second son was born in '74, followed by my daughter in '76. Even though my husband and I had a family, our marriage struggled for years until I finally had enough of an unhappy life.

When we got divorced, my children were all under 3 years old. It was scary to realize that life was going to change so dramatically. I was unsure of how to move forward, but I knew I had to for myself and my children.

Back then it was not as common to talk about, or even think about, divorce. The woman's place was still in the home, taking care of the children and the household. When I told my parents that my marriage was ending, they were in shock. They just did not understand. In their minds, a wife was just supposed to do what her husband told her and stay quiet. They were unable, or unwilling, to offer any assistance, even though they knew it was going to be very difficult for me.

Shortly after the divorce, I was forced to leave my home and had to find a place for the four of us. This seemed like an impossible task. I knew I couldn't lean on my parents or ask them for help. I felt isolated and alone and struggled with my lack of options. I didn't have a job outside the home for almost four years while I was married. I didn't have a checking account of my own or any credit in my name. Although it was a very stressful time in my life, I knew I could get through it.

I was able to get a job as a waitress, working long shifts at different restaurants to make ends meet. It was difficult to find someone who could watch my children while I worked, but I was able to procure someone for both the weekdays and weekends. At that time, I had one job to pay the bills and one to pay the babysitters.

Once I had employment, I searched the south side of Chicago for an apartment. I found one that I loved, but could not afford the three-bedroom space they had available. I then heard about a small house that I thought might work for us. I worked double shifts to get the down payment, which was only a few thousand dollars. Luckily, the bank took a chance on me, and I was able to purchase that home by myself.

I had finally secured a place to live with my 3 small children. If nothing else, we were together. And even though money was tight, things generally went smoothly for the next few years.

In the early 80's, I was frustrated with working tirelessly and not being able to spend more time with my family. I decided to get a job with Kelly Services Temp Agency in downtown Chicago, where I worked at an investment company as a secretary for a financial advisor. I immediately found that I liked working in that industry. As I gained more experience, I got a full-time position and eventually left the city to work for a firm closer to home.

In 1984 I was offered a chance to become a financial advisor in a male-dominated industry, much to the chagrin of many of the men in the office. Even my boss told me that women could never become successful advisers. Those comments made me try even harder to succeed.

I took my vacation time and spent it taking a cram course on how to pass the Series 7, the exam to receive my securities license. The first day was so hard, I came home and cried. A friend came over to encourage me to keep going, that quitting was not an option. After the course was over, I wasn't sure I could pass the 6-hour test, but I did.

It was a good thing I listened to the few people who encouraged me to move forward and not those who wanted me to give up, or those who made me think I could never be successful. After the first year of being a stockbroker, I was able to double my income and provide for my children without having to work double shifts every week. It was still a struggle to balance the time at work and the time at home, but amazing to be there much more than before.

The Second Motherhood
My second motherhood began in 1992 when I got married to the most amazing man (Jeff, 14 years my junior) who started as a co-worker and turned into my husband. He didn't have any children of his own. Mine were all teenagers when we got married. We built a house together when my youngest was a sophomore in high school. More than that, we built a life together.

We were blessed with our first child together, a daughter, who was born in 1994. Everyone already thought I was crazy to have a child in my 40's. Because I was getting older, we thought that she might be our only child. No sooner did we think that, than I found out I was pregnant again with a son who was born in 1996.

This time things were so different for me with a supportive partner. Having a loving husband who treated me like a real partner was something that I found to be very comforting. We worked together in the office as a team helping clients to build their financial futures, and we worked together at home making sure our babies were taken care of. Having help with feedings, diapers, and anything else I needed was a welcome departure from having to do it all by myself. Oh, did I mention he cooks all the meals? I have always appreciated how much he loves and cares for us.

After the children were born, I transitioned from a full-time financial advisor to a full-time mother and part-time advisor. This allowed me to be there for our children when they were young. I was able to enjoy them without the stress of being the only one responsible for everything. If the children were sick and I had to stay home, it wasn't an issue. There was someone there to take care of our clients.

My Newfound Passion

A few years later, I was able to retire from the financial industry to pursue my passion for true health. I was introduced to USANA Health Sciences shortly after losing both of my parents to degenerative diseases. I saw all their retirement funds go towards paying for medical expenses instead of what it was intended for... living their dreams. That was when I realized that your health is your most important asset. My passion changed from helping others build a financial nest egg to helping them achieve their dreams by staying healthy.

I always feel so grateful that I was able to make it through all the challenges and adversity I have faced. It has made me stronger and led me to a better life. I am happier than I ever imagined I could be, especially when I think back to the struggles that seemed so overwhelming in the 70's and early 80's. We all struggle, but should never give up on living the life we have always dreamed of living. I am living mine in happiness and health!

To those of you struggling to find that balance, in life I'd like to give you this piece of encouragement: Never give up or think you can't achieve your goals. Take daily positive actions to grow as a person during all of your challenges.

My life is a testament to the resilience and strength of women. If I can make it, you can too. Be strong, ask for help when you need it, and believe in yourself. You are capable of more than you know.

Two Motherhoods

8

A Mother's Journey from Step-Monster to Step Diva

Blending a family without going insane.

Terrie Vanover

Terrie Vanover, the Bounce Back Diva, is an Author, Speaker, and founder of Choosing to Rise, LLC. She is a divorce/family coach known for her ability to help women use their setbacks as the fuel to ignite their dreams to achieve fulfillment. After feeling powerless and completely overwhelmed by a divorce that dragged on, she was losing hope. Her struggles to be a good mother, reeling from losing her marriage, her home, and her sense of who she was didn't bury her, but instead gave her strength to prevail through the darkness. Not only that, she chose to rise above her situation and found her voice. She learned how to co-parent effectively, overcome the trials of step-motherhood, and founded her own business to help others through these transitions. She is a graduate of CoachU and holds a Master's from Concordia University. She is a presenter and has articles published all around the world and is the co-author of two women's empowerment books. She is the proud (but tired) mom/bonus mom of five children.

To learn more go to **www.ChoosingtoRise.com** or contact her at terrievanover@comcast.net

I knew that something was not quite right with my daughter from an early age. As an educator with years and years of experience working with young children, I was aware that her behavior was not typical. She struggled with sensory issues and her tantrums were overly extreme and lengthy. My husband and I contacted numerous doctors, but her diagnosis eluded us. I realized that getting help would be a long process when I arrived at a behavior specialist's appointment with my data, documentation, and a notebook of behavior logs in hand and the therapist looked at me and stated that I had already done everything that she could possibly suggest. I would need a psychiatric evaluation for her.

Was this my fault? Did I do something wrong as a mom? For months, I struggled with guilt that maybe my Caesarian section had caused issues. Of course, this was ridiculous and no amount of blaming myself would change the situation. The C-section saved our lives. Sometimes, life just isn't fair and I have come to accept that sometimes bad things happen to good people.

After psychiatric evaluations, tests, countless forms, numerous doctor calls and visits, as well as medical appointments to get a baseline of her health, we were given some information regarding her condition. While she is extremely intelligent, she has issues processing information, dyspraxia, and has difficulty regulating her moods, impulses, and emotions.

Although this was difficult to comprehend, it was a start so that we could begin to get the right therapies, the right doctors, and the correct medications. I would encourage every mother to keep the hope, keep asking questions, dig deep for strength for your child when you feel that something isn't right. If your mother's intuition is telling you that something is wrong, listen to it. Keep searching for answers... I know that it is exhausting searching for doctors, feeling unheard, feeling like you're crazy- but don't give up. Keep going. Get your baby what they need and deserve.

My daughter is creative, funny, and loving. She is an amazing actress who can imitate any accent! She is an advanced reader with strong language skills. She can be thoughtful and sweet. I want to give her all the tools and support she needs so that her wonderful qualities shine through.

After finally getting a medical diagnosis, I wanted to find support and advice from other mothers that were dealing with the grief, disappointment, and anger that I was feeling since learning about my daughter's issues. I immediately began to research books and resources to help me cope with my feelings of pain and sadness. I went to the library and began reading books for parents of special needs' children. As I read one, it spoke about the blessings of having a little one with special needs... How we should feel grateful for their differences and uniqueness.

I threw the book across the living room. NO! This was not how I felt! This was unfair!!! It's NOT FAIR that my baby would have to deal with this. It's not fair that my family has to deal with this shit.

I struggled for years and years in isolation because of my daughter's unique issues. After searching online, I finally found a couple of Facebook groups with other parents who understand the difficulties that this disorder brings. I also connected with another mother whose child struggles with these issues and it has given me hope that although the road isn't easy, there is a light at the end of the tunnel.

Unfortunately, having a special need's child, financial stress in my marriage, and my own insecurities and neediness that grew out of being raised in poverty, divorce, and being sexually molested, contributed to the demise of my own marriage. My mom did the best she could as a working-class single mom raising two young girls after a divorce with little education and little money. Being abandoned by my alcoholic father and being sexually abused by a family member when I was six led to my feelings of rejection, emptiness, shame, and the sense that I was never enough. I believe that a lot of this lack of self-worth spilled over into my marriage. I brought my own unworthiness into our relationship. I was insecure, needy, and controlling. I was a never-ending pit that could not be filled with enough love. Of course, my husband traveled frequently adding to my feelings of loneliness and isolation. The marriage began to unravel. I absolutely regret allowing my selfish needs to ruin my marriage. I hurt a man who loved me and our children more than his own life. He deserved better than how he was treated.

When we separated, I felt desperate. Those feelings of loneliness and emptiness intensified and seized me. I wanted to turn to men to make me feel wanted and loved. However, one of the hardest things and the best things I did was to force myself to just sit with those feelings of loneliness. Night after night, full of tears and heartache, I sat alone in my room with my loneliness. This forced me to come to terms with my faults, issues, and sense of abandonment. By acknowledging and accepting these issues, I was able to move forward.

Near the end of my marriage, my mother was involved in a car accident and later had a stroke. It's believed that the accident contributed to it. This stroke then paralyzed her and completely changed her- emotionally, physically, and even her personality changed. Unfortunately, my mother never recovered. She continues to deteriorate. I feel like I lost my mother when I needed her most. She could no longer talk to me or comfort me when I needed her during this dark time. She would've been a woman that understood what it was like to be going through a devastating divorce with two small children. In addition to losing my mother's support, my family was unable to give me much support since they were dealing with the daunting task of caring for my handicapped mother.

During our marital separation, my daughter seemed to ramp up her behavior. She struggled with the transitions. It was an extremely difficult time being a single mom.

Also during that time, I had no home, as my husband resided in the marital property. Luckily, a friend introduced me to someone who would change my life- her childhood friend, Kim. Kim took my two children and I into her home and gave us shelter, food, but most importantly, a sanctuary to heal during this turbulent time. She had been through a divorce and represented hope that I might be able to come out this whole and find joy again.

During training for a triathlon, I met the man who I would

later call my husband. He was athletic, sweet, charming, and easy to talk to. He was older and a friendship developed. He was also a single dad raising a boy and girl on his own. And they were teens.

Our deep friendship evolved quickly into something more. His warmth and generosity won me over. His kindness and caring, loving heart have taught me so much about what love truly is.

What I didn't know at the time was the difference in our parenting styles. I like to describe Pete as the quintessential Italian grandmother. He doted on his children and they were waited on and were always given what they wanted. They lacked responsibilities and were not given expectations that most kids their age were given.

My children were raised... differently. I believed that children should have chores and contribute to the family. My kids ate what I prepared and helped cook and clean. I had high expectations and believed that children can be self-sufficient and independent.

Over time, our kids began to spend time together and we started to discuss how we would raise our kids together. I am fortunate because Pete and I came to an agreement to how we would raise our children. We had decided to work together to have high expectations and teach the children to contribute to the household.

It was really, really difficult to blend our families. Before meeting me, Pete had come to realize that his teen age kids needed to step up and learn to be responsible for helping him around the house, but he was struggling with the transition to get them to be independent. Pete's children resisted our attempts to teach them to do even the most basic age-appropriate tasks. They didn't know how to load a dishwasher, cook a basic meal, fold clothes, do laundry or dust and vacuum their rooms. They were teenagers!! They absolutely refused to even eat meals that were healthy and balanced. Pete's kids would not even eat basic fruits and vegetables.

My young elementary aged children knew how to do more tasks than they did! I was beside myself. I was not the maid and cook for other adults. My expectations for a family is that we all pitch in and help to cook, clean, and keep our home neat.

I really felt that I could not build a family through all this resistance to even the very simplest change. Just like so many stepmothers, I felt that I was being blamed for all of the issues in the family. It was through the strength of Pete's love and his conviction that WE WOULD make our marriage work that I was able to stay through all the heartache and rejection. Pete was accepting of my children while I struggled with dealing with his children's issues. He would tell me that children will never pull us apart.

I worked with my personal coach and was able to overcome many of the issues that I was facing. Through my work with Chrissy Carew, I was able to dig down deep to uncover what was holding me back from completely trusting Pete. My mistrust stemmed from my resistance to feeling vulnerable. This breakthrough led to my relationship becoming deeper and more fulfilling with my wonderful husband. Because of my work with Chrissy, I have been able to tear down my "wall" and I have become less critical, and hence, my husband has become less defensive, allowing our marriage to flourish and grow.

With all the personal growth I have undergone and through my experiences with my life coach, I decided that I wanted to use my life to help others. I became a life coach so that I could use my life to empower women to find themselves after life's setbacks, especially divorce, to come out of it even stronger, better, a warrior! I'm here as a testament that there is hope, light, and fun after divorce and life's biggest setbacks. I have become empowered to pursue my lifelong dreams. I completed a half-marathon and a mini-triathlon! I am the co-author of two women's empowerment books, a national presenter and a contributing writer to Divorcemoms.com, MammaMia of Australia, Wellness Universe, Singlemoms.com, and Divorcemagazine.com. I founded my own business, Choosing to Rise, LLC, to help women uncover what is sabotaging them from reaching their highest potential and then help them achieve their goals.

I now co-parent 50/50 with my ex. He is engaged to marry a wonderful woman who is an incredible stepmom to my children. He is an amazing father and I'm so happy he found a wonderful partner. I feel blessed every day that she has come into their lives. She is smart, fun, thoughtful and goes above and beyond for my kids. The four of us work as a team to give all the kids what they need. We help each other out when we need to and keep our children's well-being as the focus for getting along and working together.

Although my ex and I have been able to create a positive co-parenting situation, our family has continued to face setbacks in blending our family. Pete's children went to visit their mother in another state and refused to return. His children refused to accept the changes in our family. They did not want to be a part of their baby sister's life and this hurt Pete deeply. We agonized over the decision on how to handle this.

All through these setbacks, Pete and I stood by each other and supported each other. Although things didn't turn out the way we hoped and all our hard work towards building a blended family was crushed, we have gone on to put the work into our marriage so that it is healthy and happy. We want to give the children that live with us the model of a marriage and foundation of a family that they deserve. I know that choosing a wonderful partner who would support me no matter what was the best decision that I could have made. I have known women whose partners will allow the children to disrespect them or will take the children's side when they would not listen to the stepmother. The adults (whether it is step parents or biological) need to be a united front and a team when parenting the children. If parents are struggling with this, they should seek help from a relationship coach or counselor.

The marriage is the FOUNDATION of the family. And if that foundation is rocky, the family will become unstable. I would advise any woman who is contemplating becoming a stepmother to choose a partner who will love, support, and back you up in the face of any adversity- be it his ex-wife or his disrespectful children. This is the most important factor in determining whether to move ahead in a partnership with a potential mate.

Keep searching for the partner who will love you and support you and work through the hang-ups of life- whether it's the death of a friend, negotiating the ups and downs of starting a business, or blending a family. I knew that Pete was the one for me because he was committed to doing EVERYTHING needed to make our marriage and family work.

9

Blended Family Blueprint

Tracy M. Sostand

Tracy Sostand was born in Chicago, Illinois. She has spent her life traveling between Chicago and Texas, being her father was raised there and that is where most of the Sostands reside. She lovingly refers to herself as "country girl at heart." She is from a blended family that consists of 6 other siblings from both of her parents remarrying after their divorce. She says the reason she's a well-rounded person is because, "You have to learn to be a giving person when you grow up in a blended family. It's the only way it works."

When Tracy was a student at Lindblom Technical High School, an English teacher sparked her interest in writing and pushed her to pursue it. Tracy continued to write throughout high school and college, at the same time, dancing in the company Danceworks at Chicago State University. After undergraduate school, Tracy became an educator in the Chicago Public School systems. In 2004, she was married and in 2005 became a mother. Shortly thereafter, divorced and on her own with two-year-old twins, she was faced with life as a single mother. She knew revamping her life was important, so she went back to her passion of writing. She went back to school.

She is a graduate of Chicago State University and holds an MFA in Creative Writing. She is the mother of 11-year-old twins and the bonus mother of a 22-year-old college student. In addition to being a school teacher in Chicago Public Schools for 19 years, she is a published author in this volume. Currently, Tracy is working on her solo book of short stories. In her spare time, she loves to cook and make wine and other spirits.

My mother always told me that parenting was the most fulfilling and yet challenging jobs that a woman could ever have. I watched her raise my brother and I, then she had my sister and also became a step parent to three of my stepfather's children. I watched her love and support them as if they were her own. At her funeral three years ago, I watched as my siblings and I stood and hugged and kissed mourners who loved my mother as much as we did. I also watched my siblings that she did not birth, mourn her as if she did give them life. My mother gave me a blueprint of how to love my own children, but also how to love a child that I didn't birth. She would cringe when she'd hear people say things like, "I could never love another man's child," or "that's her child, this one is mine." She said she had six children. If someone inquired further, she'd simply say, "mine, his, and ours." I know being a stepparent wasn't always easy for her, but she did it with grace and style. So when I decided to marry a man that had a child already, I figured since I grew up in a blended family, I already had a leg up, and it should be smooth sailing. I was so wrong about that.

I couldn't believe that she was calling me momma Tracy. I couldn't believe that I was going from married to married with children all in a few months. I was crazy about this kid but she was about to become my full-time responsibility in a few weeks, and I was ready to run for the hills. So I'm sitting at the kitchen table with a knot in my stomach, and my mom leans over and says, "Breathe...you've got this." I looked up at her and thought easier said than done. She looks at me and says, "You're right, easier said than done." She could always read my mind. So here I am wondering what kind of step parent I'd be. Because Lord knows my own stepfather was a force to be reckoned with. I know I couldn't look to him for a blueprint because honestly speaking, the older I got, the less he seemed to like me. To the point that I just accepted his indifference and learned to live with it. But then I did have the perfect example of how to love someone who didn't come from my own womb. My own mom.

The decision for his daughter to come to Chicago to live was to help her do better in school because she wasn't doing well at the time. I know it wasn't an easy decision for her mom to let her come stay with us, but it was about the child. We all discussed it and made the plan for her to come in June when summer school started here. So my then husband and I fly to get her, and I am nauseous all the way to Louisiana and all the way back. The trip was a breeze, meeting her mother (who I absolutely adore) and getting to know her better. Leaving the airport was the hardest. I looked at her mother, clinging to her child, and I put my arms around her and promised I'd take care of her baby, and that I'd love her like my own. At that moment, I knew that I would and could keep that promise. Little did I know what I was in for.

It wasn't just parenting. It was trying to juggle being a new wife with being a new parent and adding in a child that DID NOT want another parent. So, it started off nicely enough. We went and bought things to decorate her room, we bought new clothes, and quickly enough, settled into a routine. Of course, we had a few hiccups, a few "I want to go home to my mama," but for the most part, it was going smoothly. Then all of a sudden, after about five months, we hit a wall. She became defiant towards me; she stopped showing me affection, totally ignored me. It didn't matter what I did or didn't do; she acted like I wasn't there. Hindsight is 20-20. I now know that it correlated with her dad starting his affair and taking her around that woman. Confusion set in. And ha! So did pregnancy. Shortly thereafter, I found out I was pregnant with twins.

At the beginning of my pregnancy, she started to treat me worse. So our household was divided. They did everything together, and I was an outsider in my own home. It hurt like hell. I shared the pain with a few girlfriends, my mom, and mother in law. They were supportive but I just didn't know how to handle this situation. It wasn't going any way like I wanted it to go. I wanted to have her love and acceptance. I wanted to laugh and enjoy her the way she did with her dad. But it just wasn't happening like that. So, I gave up. Eventually, she went back to live with her mom, and I gave birth to the twins.

On her first visit after the twins were born, I wanted to hold her and not let go. It was crazy because I thought I hadn't missed her but I had. After all, in my mind, she was my first, my oldest. It didn't matter that her dad and I were on the outs and I was contemplating divorce on a daily basis. She was a big part of my heart. I showed her as much love those two weeks that I could, and hoped that she'd see that no matter what, I loved her. I think she knew that I did. It was important for her to know that because my marriage to her dad was ending and my life with the twins was about to change.

Shortly thereafter, September 2007, the divorce was finalized, and I started a life of being a single parent. Not in the sense that many say single parent. I had my every other weekend, it was nice of enough. But this wasn't supposed to be my life. I waited to have children so I WOULDN'T have to live like this, separate households with separate rules. Unfortunately, this was our life. And it was definitely challenging at times. Taking care of two babies, two toddlers, was life-altering. I wasn't eating very much, crying daily, and just looking an entire mess. My family was supportive enough, but I just couldn't get it together. Finally, my mother took me to dinner and started to talk to me, telling me that I had no choice but to get it together, and to stop looking like a hell-cat! We both cracked up laughing. And then it began, my healing. My healing so that I could parent and raise these tiny humans who didn't ask to be here.

I pulled myself together and hit the ground running. I put them in as many activities as they wanted. We tried tumbling, guitar, violin, swim, dance, Tae Kwando, and tennis. They started to grow into their own little personalities and watching them was nothing short of amazing. Any health hiccups that come with twins was long gone and before I knew it, it was kindergarten, promotion ceremonies, and black belt tournaments. And as they were growing up, so was their sister. There was 8th-grade graduation and sweet 16. She was blossoming into a beautiful young lady, and I was so happy that I was able to see her grow up. Whenever she came to visit, she spent the night with me, and we'd talk and catch up. As she's gotten older, graduating from college as this book hits the press, our relationship is phenomenal. And it's not a hint of the struggles that we endured in the beginning.

So, 14 years, a 23-year-old, and a set of 12-year-olds later,

I am still using my mother's blueprint. I love and discipline them, I encourage and correct all three of them. Because all three of them are my babies. Yes, you can love another person's child. And you can receive their love as well. My three are thriving because of it. And I have my mother to thank for that.

10

Half a Dozen, Only Children!

The importance of taking care of YOU while focusing on the uniqueness of your family.

Tricia D. Dunn

Tricia Dunn holds a dual degree in Special Education and Elementary Education. She has over 20 years combined educational experience as a classroom teacher, remedial teacher, tutor and home educator. She has the honor of being mom and teacher to her own 6 amazing children ages 8-18 as well as home educator to other students. Although Tricia's business started in 2002 with Sun Raise Academy, she recently became officially Tricia Dunn Consulting, LLC.

Tricia is passionate about helping parents discover the best schooling option that meets the needs of their individual child. She offers support and guidance in a variety of ways. Tricia is also Certified Parent Coach, Divorce Support Coach and Life Empowerment Coach.

Tricia's own experience of years of feeling like she was not living to her full potential, stuck in a people pleasing cycle and dealing with her own self-worth issues and then discovering how to break from this cycle resulted in a passion to share with others the tools needed to live empowered for life. Tricia's message is "Growth takes Time, Effort and Commitment!"

You can find out more by going to **www.triciadunn.com**
To contact Tricia, email: tricia@triciadunn.com

Healthy Mom, Healthy Family

You may have heard of the saying, "Ain't nobody happy if momma ain't happy." This is true, but it goes even a little deeper than that: healthy mom = healthy family. I married right out of college and because of people-pleasing programming, I believed that I needed to do all that I could to make everyone happy. I was very successful - so successful in fact that everyone in my life had what they needed and wanted, but I was miserable. My days consisted of getting up and barely making it through the day, doing what I had to do to take care of my children and then when their dad came home, I would go to bed or sometimes literally cry in the closet. I was depressed and having unhealthy thoughts of suicide. I put on a brave front and showed up for church activities, volunteered as a Sunday school teacher, spoke at women's meetings and supported my partner in his community involvement. The more I sacrificed and gave the more I was depleted of energy, self- worth, and my happiness. I had Super Sacrificial Mom mentality! Super Sacrificial Mom mentality is when you take it upon yourself to meet everyone's needs without taking care of your own. Have you seen any of the superhero movies? Superman, Batman, Spiderman??? Each of these civil servants have a few things in common 1. They give up/ hide their own identity 2. They have a lot of extra pressure and burden on their shoulders 3. They are isolated. Can you relate? As mom, have you forgotten who you really are? Do you take on all your family's problems (and other people's) problems – the rock of the family, the one who has all the answers? Do you feel alone... if you don't do it – nobody will? I have been here!!!! This way of living may work for a while but eventually, you will not be able to keep up with the demands you have taken on. This is what happened with me... Before my first anniversary of marriage, I was expecting my first baby fast forward a few years... and I had 6 – that's SIX babies in less than

10 years! Let's think about that for a minute – over 10 years of either being pregnant or nursing, ten years of diaper bags and baby responsibilities. I did not have a babysitter – I did not have family nearby – I was responsible for baby care, house care, husband care! In time, my self-care disappeared. Something needed to change, and it began with a realization that I was not healthy. And I don't mean just physically... in fact, I was in great physical health but as humans, we have three parts: body, mind, spirit and there are seven main areas of life that you need to tend to if you want to have a balanced healthy life.

1. Spiritual- Your inner work, healing and "self-growth" development
2. Personal- Hobbies, me time, things that you personally enjoy doing for yourself
3. Family – Family time, anything involving family and household responsibilities.
4. Health – Physical and mental health: exercise and fitness, nutrition.
5. Community – Volunteering, giving back, paying forward, contributing to society.
6. Financial – Money mindset, your income, managing and budgets.
7. Education – Continued learning about interest and developing new skills.

Each category should have about the same amount of attention... like this:

Areas of Life

- Spiritual
- Personal
- Family
- Health
- Community
- Financial
- Education

The first step to a healthy mom is to take care of yourself and bring balance back to your life. This is how my life looked!

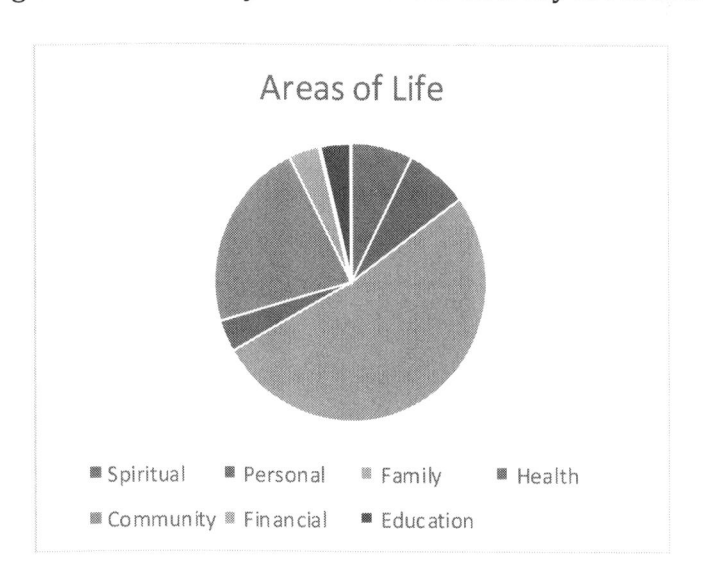

Areas of Life

- Spiritual
- Personal
- Family
- Health
- Community
- Financial
- Education

The majority of my invested time and energy was going all to my family and next to my community involvement (Volunteering, church groups and responsibilities). The other areas of life were barely my focus or sometimes not even at all. Once I saw how much the balance was off, I was able to start planning ways to put more focus in the other areas. You can check your balance by creating your own wheel with the seven areas of life. Start by asking yourself, on a scale of 1-10, one being little to no focus and 10 being the most focus, fill in your wheel. The areas that are less will be where you start to add some attention to begin to adjust your areas back to balance mode. You will find where there is balance, there is better ability to be a well- rounded, healthy super mom doing all a super mom does without sacrificing your identity, self-worth and your connection to the world around you! When you are healthy you will be happy and then a happy mom = happy home! You will be ready to take on the challenges that come and give each of the individuals in your family the mothering they need as well! This is the beauty of being a mother and the gift we possess! It truly is a superpower... By taking care of you in all areas of life, you will be able to pass that balanced way of living to your children as well!

Handling Challenges

As a single, stay at home, homeschooling mom of 6 kids, I have transitioned through several challenges, and I am going to cover a few of them and the principles I have used to move forward through them and parent my children in a healthy way. 1. Miscarriages and unexpected health concerns 2. Separation, divorce and loss of support

I had 2 young boys, both of these pregnancies were healthy and I had that feeling that I might be expecting again. I took the over the counter pregnancy test which confirmed my suspicions and I was excited to tell the news to my husband (and everyone that I saw basically!). Right away there were some things different about this one.... The major thing was I did not have any morning sickness – but why would I complain about that? I was just barely into my 2nd trimester when I started to have some spotting. That is not totally abnormal for me, but since a friend just had experienced a similar issue, I decided to get a peace of mind and a clean bill of health – I thought... instead of hearing the heartbeat and seeing a little baby heart beating (one of the most amazing, breathtaking sounds), I was told my worst fear. My baby was no longer living. I went home, and on Thanksgiving Day 2002, I miscarried. This was devastating to this day, estimated day of arrival and Thanksgiving makes me melancholy. No one can prepare you for this, and if they try it will not be as they have said because you are the one who is experiencing it and it is personal and natural to feel all the emotions that come. Years went by and I was blessed with 3 beautiful girls and was expecting my 4th daughter (my baby #6). All was well, I was looking forward to another natural birth but on the day of her arrival (my birthday of all days), it was soon clear that she was struggling to breathe – she had a lung infection. The beeps and sounds, the rushing of nurses the scary unfamiliar sights of babies under lights and the tubes!! I had entered a different world that I was not expecting. I numbly spent the rest of my two day recovery in the hospital and had to go home empty handed leaving my precious little life in the hands of the NICU nurses. We had around the clock vigil – I spent as much time as I could there, in between showing my face to my other five littles at home and pumping nonstop for when the time came for her to have something other than the fluids that she was hooked up to. NO ONE can prepare you for that. The hospital staff were amazing and cared for her as best they could but the first five days of her ten day stay were touch and go. I am blessed to say she is a very healthy almost ten year old girl today with no signs of her illness. However, those traumatic days still come and the emotions flood in.

A few years later, I would face another unexpected plan for my dream family. I was going through a divorce. I had been married almost 13 years when the process began. I had only worked outside my home the first year of marriage – no credit cards, no vehicle no family around AND 6 children ages 2-12 to take care of and provide for… this was not my plan. I am thankful I homeschooled my children because I was able to keep some sort of comfort and stability for them during an insecure time but that was about all that was consistent. Worries, concerns, fears were definitely hovering over the average parenting issues. Question: What do these have in common? Answer: These have some form of loss or fear of loss. Loss leads to grief and it is a natural part of your personal health, healing and growth. In both situations, as I was moving through the emotion process I also needed to have a plan. If I did not do so, I would have continued as a victim of circumstances and helplessness. By creating a plan, I was able to take action steps for what I could do about the situation and let go and let God step in and take care of the rest. These are the principles I still follow when new challenges arise in my family life (now I have tweenager issues, teen concerns and young adults that I am parenting and some of these challenges are troubling, but I can still hold to the principles that I will share with you now.)

1. **Create a plan**
2. **Focus on the steps you <u>can</u> do**
3. **Let go of what you cannot control and have faith**
4. **Accept the process and allow for all the emotions to come up and out for healing and health**

It is important that you realize that the outcome may not be as you planned. Anticipate the ending you would like without the expectations or the way it will unfold

This is not a magic formula for making everything better but a way to handle the challenges while you parent

Let's look at my first example of loss as an example of how I apply these four principles. My miscarriage.

1. Plan: I had a concern and made an appointment with the doctor.
2. Focus on what I can do: I decided to go home and continue the miscarriage at home. I made sure the I had the support I needed for my two young boys and me.
3. Let go and have faith: I had no choice, I had to believe that this was going to be okay.
4. Accept the process: There is no set time for grief and loss. It is personal. We honor our "Angel Lynne" twice a year and when she comes to mind. I allow for my emotions to come and go as part of my emotional healing process.

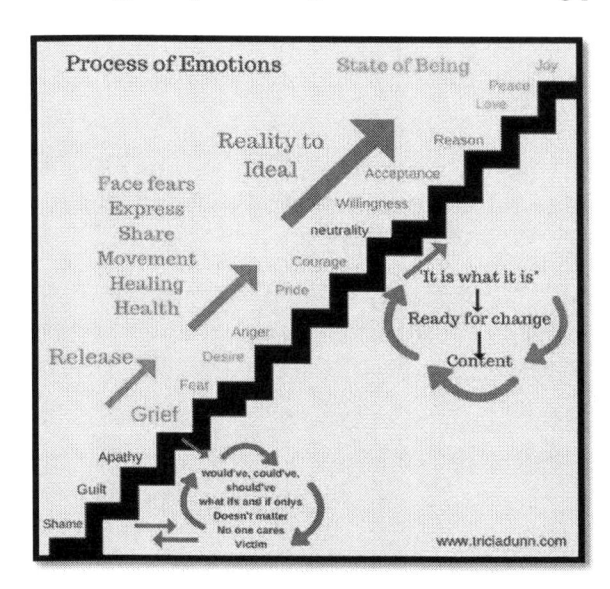

![Process of Emotions diagram showing a staircase from Shame/Guilt/Apathy at the bottom through Grief, Fear, Desire, Anger, Pride, Courage, neutrality, Willingness, Acceptance, Reason up to Love, Peace, Joy. Labels include "Reality to Ideal", "Face fears, Express, Share, Movement, Healing, Health", "Release", "It is what it is", "Ready for change", "Content", and at the bottom "would've, could've, should've, what ifs and if onlys, Doesn't matter, No one cares, Victim". www.triciadunn.com]

I do not know your circumstances; however, I do know that you will be able to handle challenges better by following these principles which will allow for you to focus on the ultimate mothering task at hand – raising healthy, independent adults.

Honoring the individuals in your family

All that my chapter has covered so far has ultimately been about being the best mother to each of your children – in my case I have half a dozen, and each of them feels like they are only children at times, and I believe that is how it should be. Whether you have 1, 6 or 14 plus, as Moms our jobs are to raise young humans to be healthy and independent. They are entrusted in our care but they do not belong to us. It is our responsibility to care, nurture, teach, correct if needed, and gently help them know how to excel at the gifts they possess and what they will add to the world. Establish three main things to nurture your child as an individual and your children will feel valued and accepted which will encourage self- confidence!

1. Understand your child and parent to their unique personality.
2. Connect with your child by effective communication.
3. Be accessible and approachable to your child.

1. **<u>Understand your child</u>**. Understanding the personality of your child will also help you in your journey as you transition into letting go and allowing for your child's independence. By understanding and accepting your child for who they are you're instilling self-worth, self-confidence, and unconditional love.
Children express different personalities from a very young age, and it will remain with them into adulthood as a unique part of them as an individual.

Recognizing these traits and embracing them as a part of what makes up your child will help you connect and develop a meaningful relationship.

	Description	Challenge	How to Parent/ Teach
Sweet	Compliant, eager to please and generally has a tender heart towards others.	As your child grows up, they may just be doing what they told and not really have any real convictions of their own.	Help your child internalize their own beliefs and opinions is key to helping him be a whole and healthy confident adult.
Delegator	Natural leader. Well-liked and likes to be in control of their surroundings. Easily passes on responsibilities.	Avoid implying that the child is "lazy" which will discourage him from doing work independently.	Help your child take responsibility for themselves and follow through with their own work.
Joyful	Bubbly and outgoing, social, optimistic and positive.	The attitudes of those around and the reality of ups and downs in life.	Help your child relate to the feelings and emotions of others around them while nurturing their innate gift of staying positive.
Resistant	Determined and knows exactly their wants. Stays with the way that works and likes what is comfortable and familiar.	The challenge is finding the balance with letting them be a true expression of self and learning how to trust and let go allowing for new experiences. Can be viewed as "Stubborn".	Avoid "the battle of the wills" and pick your battles. Provide your child with choices and options as you guide her into independence.
Laid Back	Easy going. Has the tendency to be okay with others doing things for them and making decisions.	The challenge this personality faces is avoiding manipulation and instigating of those around.	Teach the importance of expressing wants, clearly speaking and standing up for themselves is important.
Insistent	This child has a message and a point to get across. They speak loud and clear. They are persistent in making sure they are heard and understood.	Can come across as hurtful, rude or even disrespectful. When they want to express themselves, they need to do so in that instant. The challenge this personality faces is being misunderstood as uncaring for those around her and selfish.	Help them identify the feelings that others have when their words are harmful. Teach them the skill of being patient and waiting until they can communicate with their listeners with their full attention.

2. Connect with your child with effective communication

Everybody wants to be heard and feel respected and valued, and your child is no exception. One of the biggest hindrances to parenting is not connecting with your child and having an openness and trust relationship and this bond starts from the beginning. How you respond and listen to your child is extremely important to raise a happy, healthy independent adult. The best way to teach your child how you want them to respect you and the world around them is for you to MODEL this for them in how you talk and treat your child AND how you treat and talk to other people... they are always watching and learning!

5 Simple ways to improve communication with your child

1. **Relate** – Get on your child's level. See through the eyes of your child and get a clearer picture of how they view the world.
2. **Facial Expression**- Your face should match your words. Clearly explain what you are feeling.
3. **Voice**- Use a calm voice that matches the message you are communicating. Sarcasm, mocking and yelling will interfere with your message and be confusing.
4. **Touch**- Use touch to communicate gentle love and respect. Grabbing, poking, or spanking will send a negative message of inappropriate ways to interact with others.
5. **Personal Space**- Your child has needs for physical distance at times. Respect them and avoid unwanted hugs, kisses, or tickles etc...

3. Be accessible and approachable

This may seem like a demanding task and as a single mom of 6, I can tell you that it can be. The jokes about the notes and knocks at the door when you are trying to shower or use the bathroom is no joke! Children do have a knack for the most inopportune times to want to talk. One of my children loves to come upstairs and get into deep conversation when I am in the middle of work, about to get on a phone call, or just needing some time to rest. Another will want to tell important schedule changes while we are getting dinner done. This is par for the course, however, for the well-being of your child it is important to establish a relationship that encourages them to come to you any time and for any reason... Now... hold on, wait before you say – that seems a little extreme keep in mind your goal is to raise healthy, independent adults that make good choices. What I mean is you can be accessible and approachable without revolving your whole world around your child. To best be there for your children you first must take care of you and the seven areas of life we mentioned earlier. Then be there for your child in an approachable and accessible way. How is this possible?

1. **Flexibility**
2. **Quality vs. Quantity**
3. **Boundaries**

    1. **Flexibility**: Your child will feel valued and heard when you respect them. This may mean that you need to be flexible in your schedule or routine to adjust for a specific situation.
    2. **Quality vs. Quantity**: Your child wants to spend time with **YOU** – the amount of time or the amount of money spent on an activity is not as important as the quality. For example: when your toddler comes to you with a book – they may just need for you to cuddle and not looking for a whole afternoon of your time.

Just sitting in your lap and flipping through the pages may be enough to have them feel secure.

3. **Boundaries**: It is healthy for you and your children to have established boundaries. Your child needs to know how to entertain themselves and have quiet, calming alone time just as much as you do. Working this into their established routine and schedule will be beneficial in the long run. For example: My daughter and I are reading through a book together, sometimes she wants to read it with me when I cannot, and so I have already set up the boundary that if I can't do it, we schedule a time when I can. This helps her know I am not brushing her off and allows me to finish what I am doing. (The key is consistency and follow through but most importantly respect!) If you have to change the plans – let them know and reschedule just like you would a friend or another adult in your life.

When you take care of yourself, and you know how to handle the unexpected challenges you free yourself up to be a truly amazing super mom without the sacrifices and your superpower is raising super amazing humans that will grow up to be happy, healthy independent adults!

11

How to Breathe When You Have No Breath Left

Vicki Walker

Vicki Walker was born on August 7, 1966 in Chicago Illinois. She was raised by two loving middle class parents who stressed getting a good education. She attended St. Margaret of Scotland Elementary School, Academy of Our Lady High School & Columbia College where she received her degree in Journalism. After college she decided not to pursue a career in journalism right away. She started a career in Corporate America instead where she spent the next 25 years.

Over those 25 years Vicki married and had a beautiful daughter Nikki who was the love of her life. She did everything with Nikki, took her to all of her dance recitals, chess matches, girls scout outings, school plays, school concerts etc. Vicki is the President of the Smile for Nikki Foundation, which was founded on July 9, 2015 following Nikki's death.

Vicki is eternally grateful for the support that she has received for her foundation which was setup in her daughter Nikki's honor. Vicki has established a new found strength after losing her only child in a tragic accident. Through this horrible experience, Vicki has navigated her daily life by being a woman who thrives fearlessly.

Email: v.olds@smilefornikki.org
Website: www.SmileForNikki.org
Office: 219-789-1988

> *We waited and prayed for a good prognosis. At 12:53 p.m. on Monday June 1, 2015, I was told by my daughter Nikki's doctors that she was pronounced **BRAIN DEAD!!!** That kept ringing in my mind, **BRAIN DEAD!!!! BRAIN DEAD!!!!! BRAIN DEAD!!!!** I felt like Charlie Brown from the Peanuts Cartoon. What was I going to do without my Sweetpea Nikki, my daughter, my best friend and my Angel?!*

That day was the worst day of my life and I honored my Sweetpea's decision to donate her organs. She was such a loving and giving person, so what better way to give life than to preserve another's life? She saved a total of five lives including my best friend's sister Tanisha, whom I've known for over 38 years; she received her heart which was a 100% match. Nikki's organs also saved a friend of my Husband's who received one of her kidneys which also was a 100% match. My Sweetpea is gone, and yet she still lives on.

A month after Nikki's passing, two of her youth members came to me with an idea to continue her legacy. We sat in Panera Bread in South Holland IL. and on July 9, 2015, we started the "Smile for Nikki Foundation." We are a non-for-profit organization seeking to embrace others and enrich the community through the education of the performing arts, by providing training and mentorship for children in various facets of performing artistry. We enrich the minds of children ages 6-

13 by providing training and performance opportunities in the arts of dance, vocals, and acting.

I wanted to leave a note to other mothers and fathers who have lost a child or children; I know that you will never get over the pain of your loss and no one can ever know how it feels unless they have experienced it! Keep God first and foremost in your life, surround yourself with positive people who can motivate you, and just take it moment by moment, hour by hour and day by day!

Smile for Nikki Foundation

It has been three years since Nikki's passing. I'm still taking it moment by moment, hour by hour, day by day, week by week, month by month and year by year. I have been very fortunate to be involved in two major projects that have worked for me to keep me wanting to breathe and wanting to keep going since Nikki's passing. The first one that has worked for me is keeping her legacy alive through her foundation. We are going into our third season. It brings me so much joy to see the returning children from the two previous seasons and then to see the bright new faces full of life, energy, and enthusiasm to see where their talent will take them. I have two amazing co-founders, and I don't know what I would do without them. We have an amazing team of very talented professional instructors; I can't wait to start the new season. Being around the kids always takes me back to Nikki when she was here with me, about to embark on her new season of dance, a new play, or a choir concert. She was always so enthusiastic, and she was going to give 110% of herself.

Nikki got her start in dance when she was two-years-old at Studio One Dance Studio. She had a passion for dance and loved to perform in front of an audience. This is also where I found out that she had a passion for singing. They put on a talent show at the Dance Studio for their final project and Nikki sang a song by Vivian Green, mind you she was only four-years-old at the time, but she sang that song with so much passion and soul that you would've thought she was a grown woman. So when she went to Grammar School she joined the choir, and she continued to sing in choirs throughout High School and College. She was a member of the Choralteen, Vocalteen and the Velveteen Choirs in High School where she received several silver and gold medals at ISSMA. Speaking of High School, this is also where she caught the acting bug!!! A good friend of hers asked her to come try out for a part in the play they would be performing that school year. She went and got a part in the chorus of the play, and the rest was history. She performed in several plays at Merrillville High School: Phantom of the Opera, Les Miserable, Music Man, Secret Garden, Spamalot, Oklahoma, Scrooge and Cinderella where she played the Evil Stepmother. She also performed in plays at the M & M Ross Studio Theater in Hobart Indiana: Reel Horrible Night, The Haunting and Ghost Writer. To quote her drama instructor Mike Reinhart, "There was no part too small for Nikki to play." Nikki was a true Thespian.

The second project I'm involved with along with Tanisha

Aguayo was becoming Ambassadors and the Faces of the African American Community for Gift of Hope Organ & Tissue Donor Network. Gift of Hope is a federally designated non-for-profit agency that coordinates organ and tissue donation and supports families of donors in the northern three-quarters of Illinois and Northwest Indiana. Our job as Ambassadors is to go out into our communities to educate and bring awareness regarding organ and tissue donation. This also allows me to tell Nikki's and Tanisha's story, and in telling Nikki and Tanisha's story, we're educating and changing people's lives regarding organ and tissue donation. As I stated earlier in this chapter Nikki saved a total five lives with her donation, and we're continuing her legacy by the work we're doing with Gift of Hope, and she's saving more lives with her story.

Coping Mechanisms

There are a few ways I cope with the passing of my Sweetpea. I talk to Nikki all the time. When I get up in the morning I talk to her, I tell her what I'm going to do that day, I tell her how my day was and at night tell her goodnight, and that I love and miss her. Now there is another thing that I do; it's not a project, but more of a personal reminder for myself every month. It might sound crazy to some people, and my husband doesn't even understand why I do it. I set the alarm on the 1st of every month at 12:53 pm, the time of Nikki's passing, and I take a moment of silence for her. This really works for me; it gives me a sense of peace knowing that she's in a much better place! On the actual anniversary of her passing, on her birthday, and on Mother's Day, I watch the video of her homegoing service. I watch every video that I have of her performances, I watch videos that her friends made for me of her, I listen to all of her favorite spiritual songs, and I look through all of my favorite pictures of her, and I remember all of our good times we shared together and yes I cry but they're happy tears.

I know that a lot of you may be thinking, "I'm not part of any donor organization where I can go out and speak to people, or I don't have a foundation that I started in my child or children's honor, so how is this supposed to help me?" Basically what I'm saying is find that special part of your child or children that made you the happiest being a parent and embrace it. If they played sports, become a volunteer mom or dad for that sport. If they played an instrument, become a volunteer mom or dad for that. If you attend a church, see if you can start a ministry to help other parents who have lost a child or children. The most important thing is not to lose yourself because you've suffered the most excruciating pain a parent can ever experience - the loss of your child or children. I know my Angel (Nikki) didn't want that for me, so I'm sure your child or children wouldn't want that for you. You must live on so your child or children's legacy can live on inside of you!!